The Dunnavant Valley Journal

By William Boehms Norton

The Dunnavant Valley Journal
Edition One

Copyright © 2024 by William Boehms Norton
billnortonauthor@gmail.com

All rights reserved. No part of this book may be reproduced, stored in a retrieval system, or transmitted in any form or by any means—electronic, mechanical, photocopy, recording, or otherwise—without the prior written permission of the author.

Unless otherwise indicated, scripture quotations are taken from the HOLY BIBLE, NEW INTERNATIONAL VERSION ®. Copyright © 1973, 1978, 1984 by International Bible Society. Used by permission of Zondervan. All rights reserved.

Proofreader: Jill Walton, jjilleditorial@gmail.com
Designer: Clyde Adams, www.clydeadamsbooks.com

ISBN: 9798339790235

All photos by the author unless noted.
Front Cover: Double Oak Mountain from Stonegate Drive.
Back Cover: Firefighters courtesy Cahaba Valley Fire & EMR DIstrict, Sunset over Oak Mountain from Wyatts Gap courtesy Charles Wright, Locomotive at the Coosa Tunnel courtesy Chris Martin from the Birmingham Rails Archive. The Narrows postcard, circa 1940 (reference to Shades Mountain incorrect), flickr.com, no known restriction. Map, 1908 Vandiver Quadrangle, courtesy USGS.

Dedicated to the men and women of the

Cahaba Valley Fire and EMR District

and the

Dunnavant Volunteer Fire District

Contents

Acknowledgments 7
Map 8
Historical Place Names 10
Historical Key Dates 11
Introduction 12
Almost Lost Chronicles 14
    Story One: The Brits Pick a Fight 16
    Story Two: Alabama's Land Rush 19
    Story Three: The Florida Short Route 23
    Story Four: Dunnavant Past 29
    Story Five: Dunnavant Relived 36
    Story Six: The Winding Stair Trail 42
    Story Seven: By the Light of the Moon 45
Trains and Their Tracks 50
    Story Eight: Highways of Iron 52
    Story Nine: John Henry's Race 55
    Story Ten: Sounds of the Valley 59
Interlude 62
    Story Eleven: Past Yet Present 64
Life Between the Ridges 66
    Story Twelve: Rodents and Rogues 68
    Story Thirteen: Dunnavant Redux 70
    Story Fourteen: A Valentine Story 75
    Story Fifteen: Things That Prowl in the Night 79
    Story Sixteen: Firefighters Brotherhood 83
    Story Seventeen: Shoal Creek 87
    Story Eighteen: Preserving the Mountains 91
A Parting Thought 98
Appendix 100
    Walking in His Shoes 102
Endnotes 106
About the Author 110

Acknowledgments

A historical project requires wide assistance. The following were instrumental:

Junior Harris, Board Chairman for the Dunnavant Volunteer Fire District, for details from his own memories and that of other Dunnavant residents along with much-appreciated patience and encouragement,

Leland Zimmer, Shelby County Historical Society, for astute recommendations of historical materials and excellent responses to my many enquiries,

Edna Horning, for "Dunavant Redivivus" and other notes on life in mid-1900s Dunnavant,

Virginia Randolph, good friend and Dunnavant Valley historian who graciously allowed me to use her work, and

George Thompson, Thompson Realty, for Shoal Creek historical documents.

The staff of the county's periodicals, foremost being the *Shelby County Reporter*, for their excellent reporting on county events, thereby recording our history,

The Shelby County Historical Society, for its exhaustive collection of Shelby County historical documents and artifacts, carefully and thoughtfully preserved, arranged, catalogued and displayed,

The University of Alabama Libraries Map Collection for its extensive, high-quality, research-friendly map archives: www.lib.ua.edu/collections/map-collections, and

The publisher and editorial staff of *Dunnavant Valley Neighbors* for providing the valley with a unifying publication, and providing this writer a first shot at getting into print.

Jill Walton, Mt Laurel: Thorough and insightful proofreader.

Clyde Adams, Leeds: Book and map designer *par excellence*.

Last, but most influential, my wife and the best book reviewer ever: Lori.

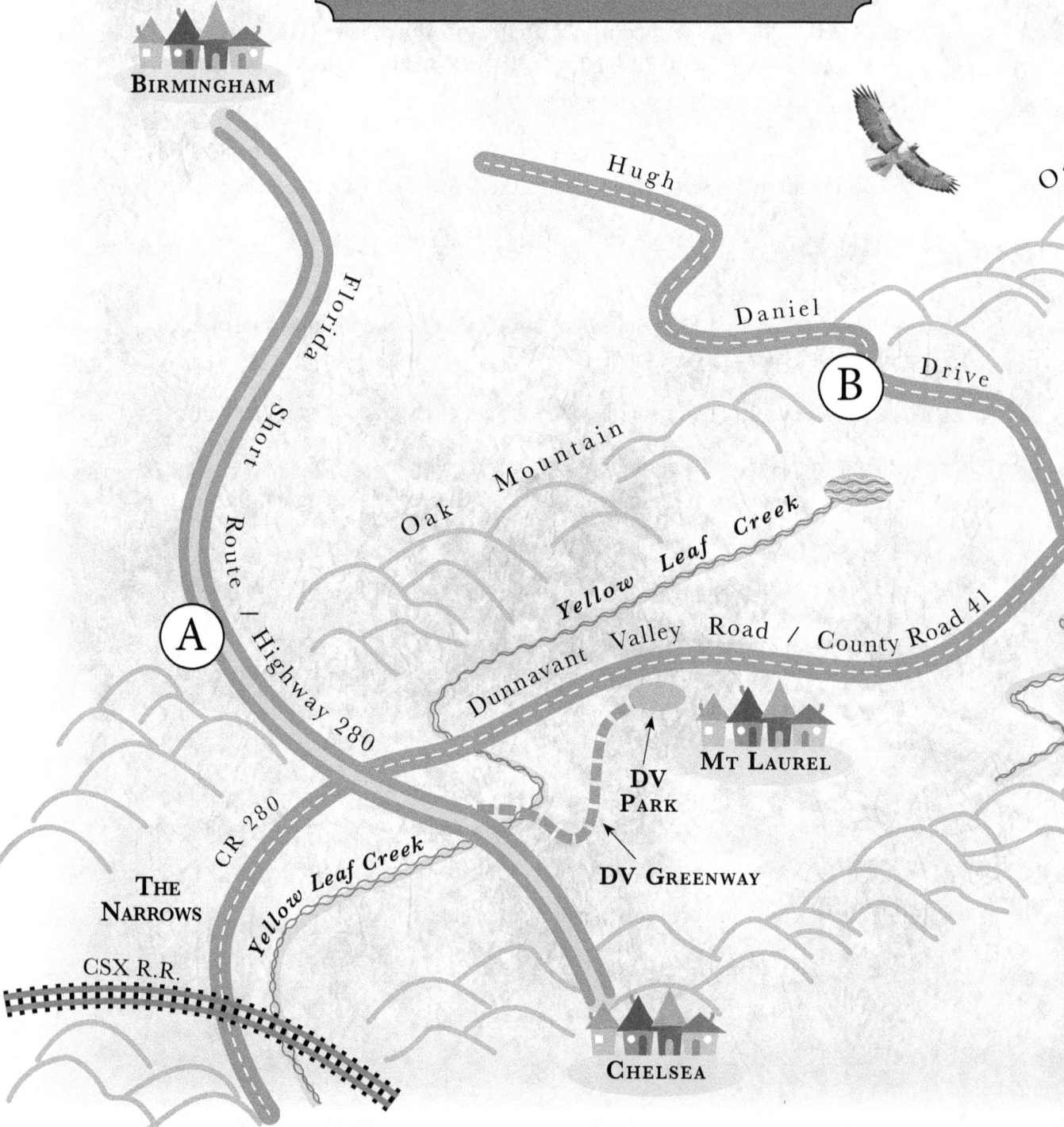

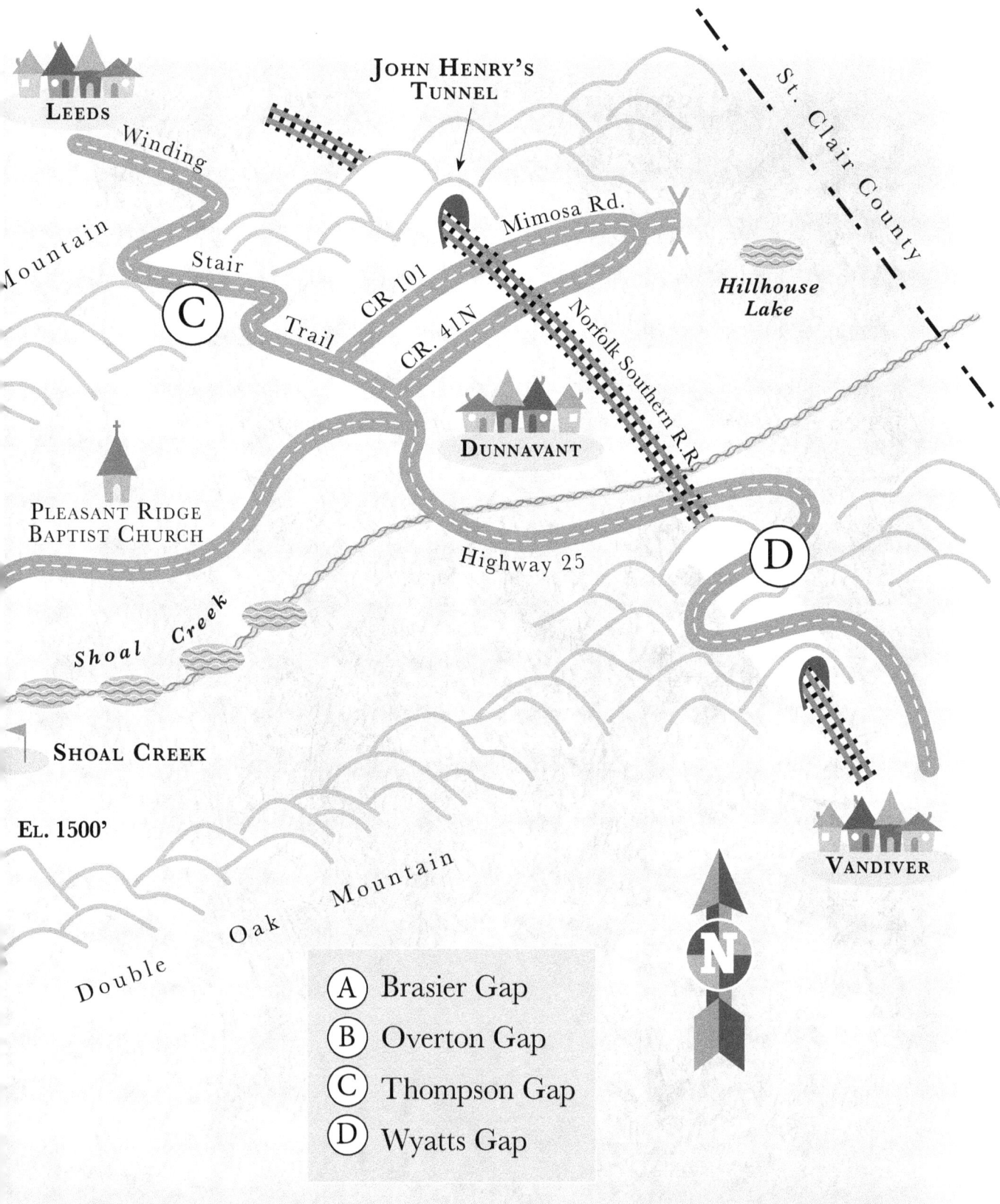

Historical Place Names

Current	Earliest to Latest
Dunnavant	Dunn & Avant Commissary
Dunnavant Valley	Shoal Creek Valley
The Narrows	Big Narrows, Little Narrows, Yellow Leaf Creek Narrows or Yellowleaf Creek Narrows
Double Oak Mountain	Bear Creek Mountain, Coosa Mountain
US Highway 280	Alabama Highway 91, Florida Short Route
Alabama Highway 25	Winding Stair Trail, Alabama Highway 21
Shelby County Road 41	Dunnavant Valley Road
Alabama Highway 119	Valley Road, Cahaba Valley Road
Norfolk Southern Railway	Columbus and Western Railway, Central of Georgia Railway, Southern Railway
Railroad Tunnels	Coosa Tunnel, Double Oak Mountain Tunnel Leeds Tunnel or Little Tunnel, Oak Mountain Tunnel

Historical Key Dates

1814
Battle of Horseshoe Bend
Gen. Jackson's Treaty Opens Alabama Settlement

1858
Dunnavant Valley Land Patents
Federal Deeds 1858-61

1892
Dunnavant on USGS Map
1887: Oak/Double Oak Tunnels
1888: C&W RR Opens

1924
Winding Stair Trail Over Double Oak Mtn
Connects Cahaba Valley-Leeds-Dunnavant-Calcis

1935
Florida Short Route B'ham-Opelika
Alabama 91 (Hwy 280)
Connects B'ham-Sylacauga-Opelika

1977
Shoal Creek, Jack Nicklaus Opens Play
Shoal Creek Country Club and Residential Community Opens

2004
Mt Laurel School
2003: Mt Laurel Hardware
2004: Elementary School

Andrew Jackson art provided by National Portrait Gallery, Smithsonian Institution
Railroad photo courtesy Charles Wright
Mt Laurel photo courtesy Cahaba Valley Fire District

Introduction

The name Dunnavant Valley does not originate from any specific family. Instead, the name comes from a railroad commissary at the north end of the valley. The story goes that the store's name combined the surnames of a Mr. Dunn and a Mr. Avant. So the area was nicknamed Dunn-Avant, and the name endured. That's the valley's tradition anyway, and I'm sticking with it—at least till a better story comes along.

Why write about the Dunnavant Valley? Because its endearing stories and natural beauty are silently slipping away. The ridgelines of Oak Mountain and Double Oak Mountain are joined at The Narrows, but then split apart as they run east toward St. Clair County. Like cupped hands, these brothers cradle the valley. Surrounded on three sides by mountains, Dunnavant Valley remained isolated long after other parts of the county developed. The uniqueness steeped in seclusion provides rich stories: ponder-provoking, inspiring, and authentic.

Isolation also meant Dunnavant Valley's natural beauty went undiscovered. The valley is carpeted with lush woodlands of white, willow, and shumard oak. Maple, sourwood, sweetgum, and hickory color the fall forest. The woodlands shelter an understory of blackberry, fringe tree, muscadine, and wildflowers. In spring, blooms of azalea, hydrangea, laurel, and dogwood decorate the forest like a dusting of snow.

Patches of longleaf pine can be found on the slopes. Once dominant across the southeast, longleaf groves are rare. On the highest ridges, some gnarled pines, oaks, and blackgums escaped logging and may be hundreds of years old.[1]

The valley's topography is mystical: it defies gravity. Somehow, the valley produces the headwaters of two streams that flow in opposite directions. Shoal Creek flows northeast from the valley into St. Clair County. Yellow Leaf Creek flows southwest into Shelby County.

The topography is rugged, too. The valley is accessible by primary roads at only three points: the Florida Short Route (US Highway 280), Hugh Daniel Drive, and the Winding Stair Trail (Alabama Highway 25). At the northern end of the valley, a rail line cuts through two tunnels that were hewn out of solid rock in the late 1800s.

Dunnavant Valley is indeed a unique and beautiful place. But the secret is out: Development threatens to overwhelm the very attributes that make the valley so attractive.

The valley marks the southernmost tip of the Appalachian Mountains. In fact, negotiating Hugh Daniel Drive reminds this Tennessee-bred boy of the forest-enveloped trails of the Smoky Mountains. I almost expect a black bear to scurry by. Dunnavant Valley is a last little gift from that old mountain chain.

What follows are eighteen true stories written about or inspired by the valley.

I hope you enjoy them.

—Bill Norton
Dunnavant Valley, Alabama, August 2024

Almost Lost Chronicles

Stand at the crossroads and look;
Ask for the ancient paths,
Ask where the good way is, and walk in it.
—Jeremiah 6:16

Story One

The Brits Pick a Fight

Three decades after surrendering their American colonies, the British were having second thoughts. The War of 1812 between Britain and the United States—sometimes referred to as the "Second War of Independence"—originated with British harassment of American merchant ships. Native American attacks on frontier settlements—incited and supplied by Britain—were a contributing factor.

The British with their bases in North America and fearsome, 1,000-ship navy could attack America directly. During the course of the war, they ransacked Washington, DC, and burned the White House. In late 1814, the British occupied half of Maine and dubbed it "New Ireland."

The Americans could not get to Britain proper, so they did the next best thing—they attacked the British colony of Canada. Many American leaders wanted to annex Canada and drive the British from the continent. They assumed Canadians would look on the invaders as liberators. They did not. (It was for the best. They play hockey; we love football. It would never have worked out.)

In the Mississippi territory (which included the future state of Alabama), British agents encouraged factions of the Creek tribe of Native Americans to attack American settlers. A full-on civil war erupted between Creeks who were favorable toward the Americans and those who were not. With their history of conflict with the Creeks and their fear of Britain's Native American allies to the north, Tennesseans took the lead to respond to the violence. And so, Major General Andrew Jackson entered the history of Alabama.

General Jackson's aggressive intervention led to the Battle of Horseshoe Bend on March 27, 1814. Horseshoe Bend is a U-shaped crook in the Tallapoosa River, near present day Daviston, Alabama, in what was a hostile wilderness.

In this battle, Jackson commanded 2,700 Tennessee militia and regular US Army. The militia and army forces were joined by about 600 friendly Creek and Cherokee fighters. Against this force stood approximately 1,000 Creek warriors determined to preserve their traditional way of life. They were known by their red-painted war clubs, the infamous "Red Sticks."[1]

Only about one third of the Red Sticks were armed with muskets or rifles, the rest fought with bows and arrows, knives, and war clubs. The Red Sticks's ferocity all but made up for being outnumbered and outgunned. The bloody hand-to-hand battle raged five hours. Between 800 and 900 Red Stick warriors lay dead when their leader, Menawa, himself wounded several times, escaped with the few survivors. The defeated Creeks fled south to seek refuge in Spanish-controlled Florida.

Jackson's forces suffered 202 dead and wounded. The wounded included Private Sam Houston, future founder and first president of the Republic of Texas. A scout for Jackson's expedition was Davy Crockett who would die in Texas at the Alamo. At the conclusion of the War of 1812, General Jackson would lead another mixed army to defeat the British at New Orleans.

The terms of the 1814 treaty ending the Red Stick uprising required over twenty million acres of Creek and Cherokee land to be relinquished by both rebellious and friendly tribes, including those allied with the Americans. This vast swath of land would ultimately form nearly three-fifths of present-day Alabama. The Creek tribes were forced into areas east of the Coosa River releasing the interior of the future Alabama to pioneer settlement—including what is now Shelby County and its Dunnavant Valley.

How would the future of the Mississippi Territory have been shaped if Britain had not picked a fight with the US? Who knows, but Tennessean and future president Andrew Jackson decided the issue for Alabama.

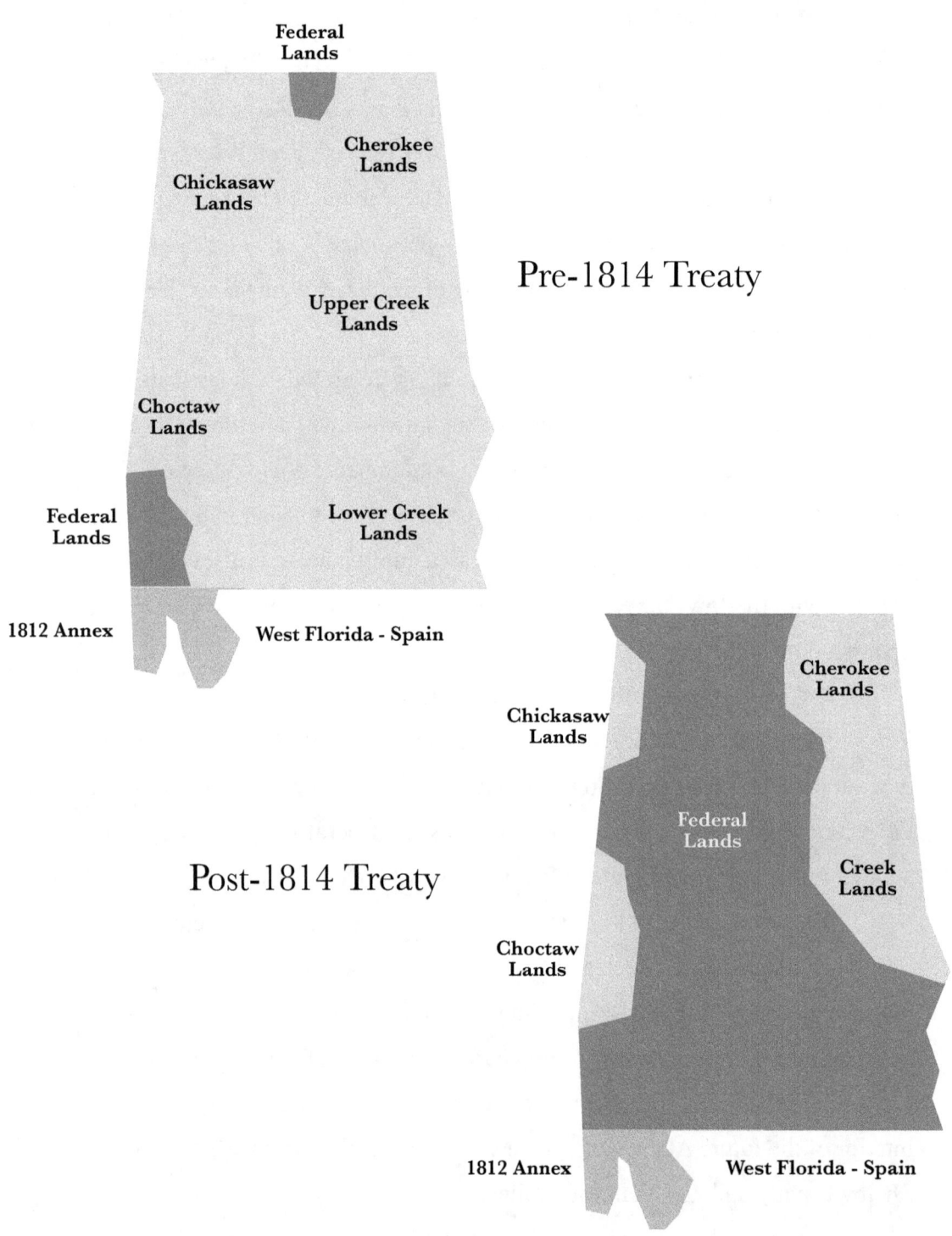

Developed from: Map of Alabama, 1818, *John Melish; www.loc.goc/item/2012590211/, and* Wikipedia, *"Mississippi Territory," August 2024; en.wikipedia.org/wiki/Mississippi_Territory*

Story Two

Alabama's Land Rush

A flood of settlers entered Alabama soon after the treaty with the Creeks was signed in 1814. This rush for land has been referred to as "Alabama Fever." Because of the Appalachian ridgelines that run northeast to southwest across Alabama, many settlers of Shelby County arrived by traveling along the Coosa and Cahaba River Valleys, which flow southwest between the ridges. The major towns of Shelby County—Wilson's Hill (Montevallo), Shelbyville (Pelham), Harpersville, and Wilsonville—were established in or near the river valleys.

The Dunnavant Valley, at the time known as the Shoal Creek Valley,[1] does not contain a major waterway. The mountains creating the valley form a wishbone shape: the two prongs are Oak and Double Oak Mountains which join at The Narrows to form the base of the wishbone. The two prongs open to the northeast toward today's St. Clair County. Settlers entered the valley by two means: Either climbing over the mountains or through the open end of the wishbone using the longer but more walkable route.

All of the land surrendered by the Creeks in 1814 immediately became federal property. Early settlers held their lands by squatters' rights; title to their holdings in the form of a land patent—similar in function to a deed—was issued by a federal land office. Whoever secured title from the land office first was the legal owner.

Put yourself in the place of the settlers scrambling for land after the 1814 treaty. First, the settler had to get to Shelby County through dangerous wilderness. Stragglers from the Creek tribe could still be about, and they would be unhappy to have lost their land. Wild animals and harsh weather would be a constant threat.

Roads were limited. According to the *State of Alabama Highway Department, Historic Roads and Trails* map, two roads ran from North Alabama to Tuscaloosa: Byler Road (1819) and Bear Meat Cabin Road (1818). These roads ran through today's Jefferson County but neither entered Shelby County. General Jackson's military road from Tennessee to Horseshoe Bend (1813-14) ran along the Coosa River. This road would have been close to several of the early Shelby County settlements.[2]

One must understand that "road" meant trees were cut, boulders moved, and stream fords had been found. Features by which we define a road today, earthmoving and bridges for example, were primitive at best.

The *Historic Roads and Trails* map also identifies an unnamed east-west Indian trail across Shelby County to Tuscaloosa. And it also marked the Pensacola Trading Trail running north-south along the Coosa. Many unmapped hunting trails certainly crisscrossed Shelby County. In 1814 or 1815, Joseph Ray, a Tennessean who appears on General Jackson's muster roll,[3] moved his family and household goods on pack horses into Shelby County. His path was an "Indian trail that led from Ditto's Landing to Mud Town on the Cahaba River."[4]

However, the search to find a specific piece of land would involve leaving trails and roads and hacking through trackless virgin forest. The difficulty of travel for early settlers cannot be overstated.

Okay, say the settler finds a nice plot that looks like rich farmland, just where is it? To claim the land, it must be located using the section, range, and township grid which overlaid Alabama but was unmarked on the ground. Surveying was just beginning and markers were limited. Hand drawn maps using whatever landmarks were at hand would have to be used to prove and locate the claim at the land office. It is reasonable to assume the perimeter of the claim would be marked with stone monuments or tree cuttings.

Beginning in 1820, the land office serving Shelby County was located in "Tuskaloosa," which was some thirty to sixty miles away from sites in Shelby County. No communication system existed other than walking. Claims had to be made in person at the land office. Another stroll in the wild. (Prior to 1820, the land office covering Shelby County was located in Nashville.) [5]

The settler's absence brings up the problem of interlopers: squatters coming later or others with less scruples that might contest a claim. Settlers would naturally be in groups, such as adult family members, to better defend their land.

Today, we cringe at this long, dangerous, and physically difficult process to find and gain title to land (closing attorneys were way off in the future). But at the time it was more than worth it: land constituted food, economic independence, and any hope of wealth.

For the Cahaba River Valley, *The Family Maps of Shelby County, Alabama* records that federal land patents were issued extensively in the 1820s.[6] Federal land grants for the Cahaba River Valley in the *Old Tuskaloosa Land Office Records & Military Warrants 1821-1855* also appear in the 1820s.[7]

For the Dunnavant Valley, a different story unfolds. With some exceptions, land patents or grants in the valley do not appear until 1858. The valley was certainly inhabited prior to 1858. The sudden change implies the federal government began a process at that time to record land claims for settlers already living in the valley.

Alabama seceded from the union on January 11, 1861, and land patents in the Dunnavant Valley ceased between January 1861 and 1885.[8] It would make sense that the federal government turned off the land spigot as a result of the war.

Cotton and Coal

The attraction of inexpensive land brought settlers from Tennessee, Georgia, and the Carolinas to Alabama. The level and fertile river valleys of Shelby County were well suited to large-scale farming, including cotton planting.

The mountainous areas of the county did not experience this type of agriculture-fueled growth. The topography was more favorable to smaller, family-owned farms. The Cumberland Gap National Park website explains:

> Survival in the southern mountains meant living off the land. Between the mountain ridges, the valleys were much more fertile and better to farm. Wild plants served to cure many of the more common mountain ailments and crops such as corn and sorghum were staples of the people that lived throughout the region. Hogs, sheep, chickens, and some cattle provided food, milk, and eggs. All activities were generally geared toward survival.[9]

The southern Shelby County agricultural economy was augmented by the discovery of iron ore and coal deposits which led to a booming iron industry. This industry was important to the South's Civil War effort, and Shelby County iron plate was used on Confederate ironclad ships.[10] After the war, the iron works at Shelby were rebuilt and operated up to 1923.

The Dunnavant Valley lacked mineral deposits. So it missed both the cotton influx and the iron boom. Like a small piece of Appalachia, life continued without interference for generations.

The future boom that the Dunnavant Valley would not miss was the need for suburbs for Birmingham. But that gets ahead of the story.

Story Three

The Florida Short Route

Imagine all the development along the US Highway 280 corridor—including those annoying red lights—turns to gray dust and blows away. In the view south from the Summit, thick forests dominate the landscape all the way to the mountain crests on the horizon. Herds of white-tailed deer and flocks of wild turkey roam the forests along with black bears and bobcats and perhaps even a panther. A white mist lies above the Cahaba River.

This vision seems farfetched; it's hard to imagine, but the busy thoroughfare we call "280" was a late addition to the road system of Alabama.

The geography of northern Shelby County is characterized by the southernmost arms of the Appalachian Mountains. During the mid-1800s, no easy route existed to travel southeast from Elyton (the future Birmingham) through these ridges. Road and railroad progress through the ridges defined the direction of development in east-central Alabama.

In 1873, a cholera outbreak almost wiped out the new city of Birmingham, but soon thereafter Birmingham began a period of explosive industrial growth. In 1871, the population stood at some 1,200, but in twenty years the population burgeoned to 26,000 earning Birmingham a nickname: the Magic City. This growth and fear of another epidemic spurred the development of a new source for city water. The Cahaba Pumping Station was constructed in 1890 on the Cahaba River to move water by pipeline to the treatment plant on Shades Mountain. Mr. W. A. Merkel was the engineer for the project.[1]

The pumps and station equipment arrived in Birmingham by rail and were hauled to the site on a newly built road by teams of six oxen. The road to the pump station was called Pump House Road (engineers are not known for creative naming), and the village built to house the workmen was named New Merkel. The village later became today's Cahaba Heights.

The significance of this story is that Birmingham was then connected by road with the Cahaba River Valley across the steep ridges of Red Mountain and Shades Mountain. However, travel further south was opposed by Oak Mountain, Double Oak Mountain (first known as Bear Creek Mountain), and the twin ridges of Double Mountain.

Some forty-five years would be required to have a safe, all-weather, state-maintained route from the Cahaba Valley through the mountains to the towns of southeast Alabama. But that was not for want of trying. Let's review the attempts to get beyond the ridges.

1890: The US Geologic Survey (USGS) map shows routes over Oak Mountain at Lowry's Gap and Shepherds Gap.[2] These "roads" were not for the faint of heart: climbs of over 600 feet were required with slopes almost twice as steep as today's Hugh Daniel Drive. These routes were probably created for logging or hauling lumber from sawmills. Old logging roads or "skid trails"—some have been promoted to "jeep trails"—crisscross the ridgelines even today.

Early 1900s: Local sources say that to get from Chelsea to Birmingham, other than with a railroad ticket, required hitching a team and taking timber roads to Pelham, which had a road north parallel to the Louisville and Nashville Railroad. By these paths, Chelsea was some forty tedious road miles from Birmingham. During wet or wintry weather even that access was unavailable.[3]

One non-mountain road accessed Dunnavant. Hillhouse Lake Road followed the same route from St. Clair County that the original settlers used. Sometime between 1998 and 2004, Hillhouse Lake Road was closed to the public and a locked gate installed. How can a public road be made private? Perhaps it was never public. Early roads were often built and owned by private individuals or companies, rather than the government. For example, Highway 25 originated as a private road.

Nevertheless, the closing of Hillhouse Lake Road removed access to Harmony Church Cemetery, which contains the final resting place of ancestors of current Dunnavant residents.

Early 1920s: According to local sources, a group of concerned Chelsea farmers, anxious to get farm products to market, took matters into their own hands. The farmers used their tractors to grade a road over the mountains to connect Chelsea with Valley Road (now Cahaba Valley Road or Highway 119). By crossing the Cahaba River, perhaps at Caldwell ford, this route would take the determined traveler to New Merkle. This cut the road distance from Chelsea to Birmingham by half.[4]

However, this convoluted path is unlikely to have cut travel time by the same amount. And given that this route still went over the mountains, the slopes involved would be nail-biters.

1926: *The Shelby County Road Map*, prepared by Mr. E. A. Turner for the county board of revenue, has a large empty area, some nineteen miles long, between Pelham and Dunnavant without a single north-south through-road. The area between Valley Road and Chelsea is simply blank. This map documents that no official government route through the mountains existed.[5]

So we're up to about 1930 and the mountains are decidedly winning. What finally got us through the mountains? Simple: politics.

Good Roads for All

During the early 1900s, the automobile was becoming a means of long-distance transportation—that is, where roads were available. From about 1880 till the 1920s, farmers, bicycle clubs, and in particular, towns that did not have railroad access, pushed nationally for the construction of all-weather, long-distance roads.

The National Highways Association (NHA) was established in 1911 to promote the development of an improved national road network under the slogan

"Good roads for everyone!" The "Good Roads Movement" became so powerful that its endorsement of candidates decided elections.

The political pressure became intense for construction of a state road southeast from Birmingham through the mountains to Sylacauga where it would join US Highway 241 and continue to Opelika. The route used Brasier Gap to cross Oak Mountain, but through Double Oak Mountain and Double Mountain the route followed two rugged gorges. The names of the gorges are "Big Narrows" and "Yellow Leaf Narrows" on USGS maps. But locals called the entire area simply "The Narrows."

The Narrows

The North Fork of Yellow Leaf Creek joins with the Ivy Branch and flows out of the south end of Dunnavant Valley. In its struggle to get to Chelsea, the stream cut through the intervening ridges by creating rock-faced, constricted canyons.

Before a road shared The Narrows with Yellow Leaf Creek, the chasm offered a quiet, sheltered, wooded retreat along a babbling, clear mountain stream. It was a place for family gatherings and church picnics and a comfortable spot for a young man to court a young lady. Many contemporary sources designate it as one of the most beautiful settings in central Alabama.[6] *The Birmingham News* reported concern over a four-lane Highway 280 before it was announced it would bypass The Narrows:

> When word got out that the highway [280] was to be four-laned, it worried people who thought The Narrows was about the most attractive gorge in Alabama. Its sheer rock walls, foliage and the tumbling waters of the creek drew nature lovers and artists in the spring and fall.[7]

Road work to create Alabama Highway 91 began in either late 1929 or in 1930—the *State Road Map of Alabama 1930* shows the stretch as "projected."[8] The Narrows portion of the project was a struggle, making slow progress for a distance of only two and a half miles. The work was done by convict and Works Progress Administration (WPA) labor using mule teams.[9] Extensive blasting was required using laborious hand-operated drills and dynamite. The quaint stone wall along the creek is typical of WPA or Civilian Conservation Corps projects.

The *State Road Map of Alabama 1934* indicates Highway 91 was paved to Westover but the segment to Harpersville was still under construction.[10] The road from Birmingham through Harpersville and on to Sylacauga was finally completed in 1935, albeit several segments were chert or gravel.

Paving the highway from Birmingham all the way to Auburn was not completed until 1941. My generation waited with anticipation for the route to become four-lane; we took paving for granted. Not so for the previous generation, they longed for basic tarmac.

Alabama Highway 91 was sometimes called "War Eagle Highway" because it provided a direct route (via Opelika) to Auburn. It also earned a grim name tag: "Blood Bucket Road." It was considered one of Alabama's more hazardous routes due to traffic accidents along the stretches of narrow two-lane roadway. The Narrows certainly had a part in the epithet: At the north end of the gorge is a rock face that earned the title "Killer Rock" because of those who died taking the curve too fast.[11]

Alcohol might have been involved. National prohibition ended in 1933, but Shelby County was "dry," that is, alcohol sales were prohibited, into the 1970s. In neighboring Jefferson County, however, sales of alcoholic spirits were legal.

A local resident reports that drinking "clubs" operated in Jefferson County just over the line from Shelby County. The joints lined Highway 91 (today's Cahaba River Road) from the Cahaba River to Cahaba Heights. The clubs sported names like Clover Club, Miami Club, Twin Pines Club, Ben's Barn, and Cahaba Cave.

Club imbibers headed home to Shelby County risked fatal consequences in the curves of The Narrows.

The Florida Short Route

Prior to the invention of air conditioning, Florida was a sweltering, mosquito-laden, alligator-infested wasteland (or so Northerners assumed). But after air conditioning was invented in 1902, Florida gradually became a vacation spot for the eastern half of the US.

Alabama Highway 91 to Sylacauga shortened travel time to Florida from the Midwest. Hence, the name "Florida Short Route" was coined as a promotion to lure tourist traffic through Alabama.[12] The name was used for the highway almost from its inception and may be found on old maps showing the original route. (Curiously, "Florida Short Route" also appears along a county road between Harpersville and Wilsonville on the 1926 E. A. Turner map mentioned above.)

In 1953, the federal government took over Alabama Highway 91 to improve maintenance and provide a continuous federal highway all the way to east Georgia. The feds treated the route as a spur of US Highway 80, a cross-country route that runs east-west across Alabama through Montgomery. The feds added a "2" to "80" and that is how the Florida Short Route acquired the official moniker of "Highway 280" that we use today.[13]

The segments of the original two-lane route that are still in use have been renamed and their origin forgotten. For example, Cahaba River Road—which once transported patrons of the Clover Club—was originally part of the Florida Short Route. Other segments carry the colorless name Old Highway 280. Retaining Florida Short Route or even Old Highway 91 would have preserved the history.

Before Highway 280, development southeast of Birmingham was blocked by parallel ranks of steep ridges. The Dunnavant Valley was isolated; it might as well have been in Kentucky. When the mountains were breached by Highway 280, it changed the future for the beautiful and secluded Dunnavant Valley.

Story Four

Dunnavant Past

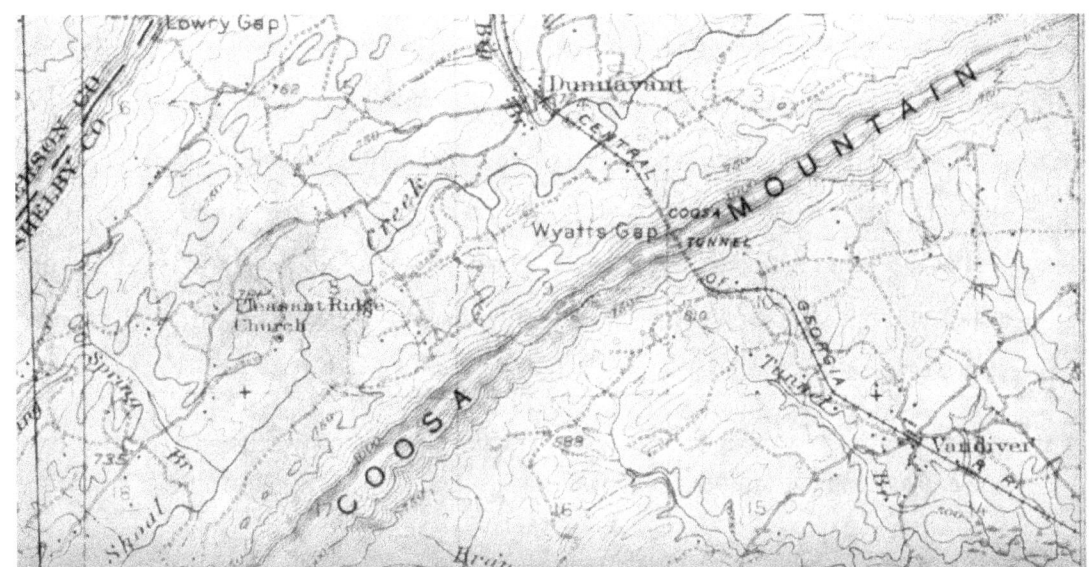

Courtesy USGS 1908 Vandiver Quadrangle

The family name Dunnavant does not appear in the *Alabama Ancestral Homesteads*[1] for northeastern Shelby County nor in the Shelby County Historical Society's *Surname File*.[2] Nor are there variations such as Dunavant, Dunivant, or Dunnivant. Further, these names are not listed in General Jackson's muster roll or Civil War muster roles relative to Shelby County.[3] Nor do these names appear in the land grant warrants or land patents of northeast Shelby County in the 1800s. Many towns were named after early settlers, but this does not appear to be true of Dunnavant. (The 1890 national census would have been helpful with this question but according to the National Archives that particular census was destroyed by fire.)

The Heritage of Shelby County, Alabama, a comprehensive history of Shelby County, says the name originated from a railroad commissary that served work crews when the Columbus and Western Railway ran its track across Dunnavant Valley in the late 1880s.[4] Imagine an unpainted wooden shack with a black stove pipe out the top or maybe it was a large canvas tent with a plank floor.

The *Heritage* reports that the store was named after its two proprietors: Mr. Dunn and Mr. Avant. The Southerner pronounces Dunn and Avant's as "Dunn 'n' Avant's," or simply Dunnavant's. It is easy to surmise that the community that coalesced around the railroad picked up the name of this enterprise and it remained when the namesakes moved on to the next construction camp. Locals favor this origin of the name.

"Dunnavant" first appears on a USGS map in 1892, just a few years after the railroad through the mountains was finished in 1888. So the timing tends to agree that the name is tied to the railroad. The name was subsequently extended to the entire valley of which Dunnavant was the first settlement. Prior to 1892, maps referred to the valley as Shoal Creek Valley.

The earliest map to show the community was the USGS map of 1892 and the spelling was Dunnavant. *The Heritage of Shelby County, Alabama* notes that the name is misspelled "Dunavant" (one "n") on an unspecified highway map.

In fact, the Alabama Department of Transportation (ALDOT) on its *General Highway Map of Shelby County*[5] uses the single "n" spelling. But ALDOT contradicts itself: the *Highway Functional Classification*[6] map uses the double "n" spelling. Further, when the community was shown on official Alabama Highway Department maps, 1957-1962, the spelling was Dunnavant.

To make the issue more baffling, other sources spell the name different ways. Rand McNally's 1890s railroad maps of Alabama spell the community with a single "n." However, in an 1898 map (first copyrighted 1895), Rand McNally changed its mind and spelled the community Dunnavant.[7]

Confused yet?

To reach a conclusion, consider local authorities and current usage: Maps issued by Shelby County (including the GIS maps) and the Shelby County Chamber of Commerce, Carto-Craft maps, the county historians who wrote *Heritage*, and local place names and residents use the spelling "Dunnavant."

Regardless of the confused past, today it's Dunnavant.

Early History

The Dunnavant Community Cemetery listing (compiled by the Shelby County Historical Society in 1979) identifies some of the pioneering families in the Dunnavant Valley as Alexander, Adams, Bowdoin, Batton, Harris, Brasher, Parker, Ramey, and, outnumbering them all, Isbell (also spelled Isbil).

Employing the FindaGrave website, the oldest marked interments in the area can be determined.[8] In the Kendrick Cemetery, it is John J. Dorough, who died in 1883. In the Harmony Church Cemetery, it is Rebecca Watts Isbell, who passed in 1874. The oldest known interment in the valley is in the Dunnavant Community Cemetery: Elizabeth Isbell who died in 1861. Families were living and dying in the Shoal Creek Valley long before Dunn and Avant's Commissary contributed the current name.

The Civil War years, 1861-1865, devastated the South including Shelby County. The iron industry of the county based in the towns of Columbiana and Shelby was destroyed by Wilson's raiders on March 31, 1865. Wilson would go on to destroy the South's military facilities in Montevallo and Selma, burn the University of Alabama, and occupy Montgomery.

There is no record that the Dunnavant Valley saw any battles, but it shared in the poverty that followed the war. With industry ravaged, no jobs, no money to restart farming, no farm animals, and many families without men, hunger stalked the citizens of Shelby County. Horses were scarce and people traveled by walking. For some time, the church was the only institution still standing: it offered hope, comfort, and prompted the sharing of food and clothing.

The rebuilding and expansion of the railroads after the war gradually brought economic activity back to the county. Because of its isolation, recovery would be slower in the Dunnavant Valley. However, with the construction of the Columbus and Western Railway across the north end of the valley in 1888, this began to change.

At various times between 1886 and 1926, the peak of the logging industry in the county, temporary logging rail lines operated in Sterrett, Longview, Westover, Wilsonville, Maylene, and Saginaw.[9] During this period, a spur rail line was laid from Dunnavant into the hills behind Pleasant Ridge Baptist Church and from Chelsea into The Narrows.[10] By these two rail lines at opposite ends of the valley, the timber in Dunnavant Valley was harvested, and the tree canopy today is a second growth forest. For reference, some two-thirds of the Smoky Mountains were clear cut—with trees being harvested as late as 1939—and the forests have recovered in the eighty years since.[11] The timber from the valley was used for lumber to build the rapidly growing towns and cities of Alabama and for the creosote-treated ties and trestles of the railroads.

In the first half of the 1900s, Dunnavant and the nearby village of Milburn shared a rail depot with several passenger train stops per day. It's inconceivable today, but Leeds and even Birmingham were accessible by train for shopping. In the 1920s, a Dunnavant resident of the time reported that a shopper could leave Dunnavant for Leeds at 11:00 and return by 3:00.[12]

In 1919, Dunnavant had a rural free delivery route operating out of its post office.[13] The Dunnavant Elementary School, which opened in 1923, held classes in a three-room wood-frame building near where the current Community Center is located.

In 1924, a private road nicknamed the "Winding Stair Trail" was completed through Dunnavant to the Cahaba Valley. Alabama developed this route into state Highway 25 in 1930. Dunnavant was then connected by a "good" road with Leeds to the north and Harpersville to the south.

In 1934, Alabama Highway 91 (later US Highway 280) was routed through The Narrows and opened up the southern end of Dunnavant Valley. Dunnavant was then connected by a state-maintained road with Chelsea and Birmingham.

During this time, Dunnavant Valley Road was a narrow country lane winding through the woods. A portion of the original route, labeled Old Dunnavant Valley Road, is located about a half mile south of Mt Laurel.

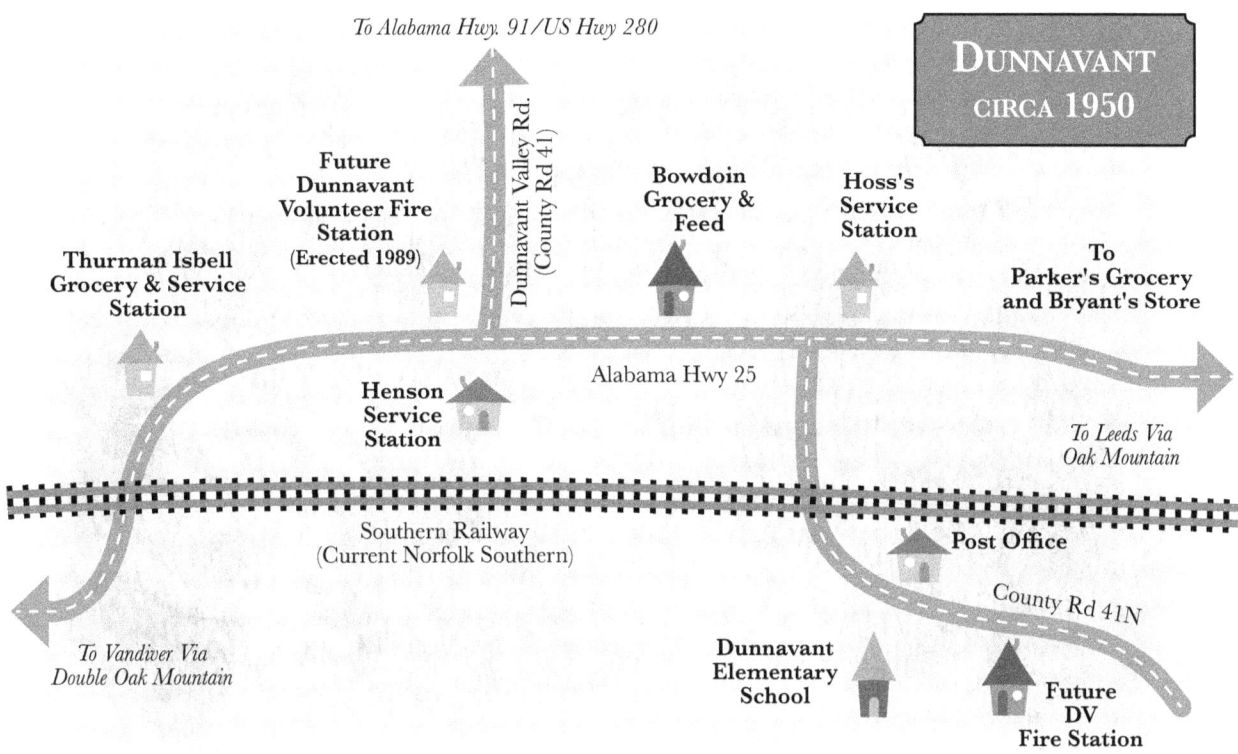

(Construction on the current route, now designated County Road 41, was started in 1961 and paved in Spring 1962.)[14]

Dunnavant became a notable crossroads of northeast Shelby County. It was a bustling little community with five stores and three filling stations. It was a magic time between engagement with the world outside the valley, but before the new roads led to Walmart and Target.

Subdivision development in the valley was not even conceived, yet.

Generations

Historical records are limited for Dunnavant and the valley named for it. But from the earliest times, the Dunnavant community was always about family.

Pioneer survival was literally based on the family co-laboring together through good times and bad. Faith in God underlay the loyalty to each other and provided perseverance in hardship.

The Giles Frontier website describes pioneer family life in this way:

> . . . the family relationship was the heart of pioneer life. It had to be. They depended on each other, sometimes for their very own survival in a time of great sacrifice and danger. They were their main source of socialization and education, too. Older siblings cared for younger siblings; younger siblings looked up to older siblings. . . . Reunions and Christmas were important traditions if you could leave your crops to go. Reunions instilled a sense of pride in family, cousins, and distant kin. Family names and keeping ties with family was important, no matter how far away they lived or how far down the genetic line they were.[15]

I can identify with this account because I experienced it growing up in a large but close extended family in middle Tennessee.

Jerrold Parker was one of five siblings who grew up in 1930-40s Dunnavant. He related his family experience as follows:

> Something memorable would always happen at the famous family gatherings—the "Parkers Get Togethers in the Grove" with Emmett's barbeque and Catherine's famous sauce. . . . the heritage of those great eating, sharing, and afternoon baseball games in the pasture stand out as wonderful events in my life.

> May the Lord bless all of you who read these words and realize they come from the heart of an individual who is truly thankful for the family from which I have sprung.[16]

Some Dunnavant families—the Harris, Parker, and Isbell families to name a few—have lived in Dunnavant for generations. The Harris clan can trace its lineage back to the first settlers in Dunnavant Valley. Four generations of Harris families have been born in Dunnavant. Even today the Harris family has reunions and Christmas gatherings every year and dinners on Sundays. The settler spirit of kinship is alive and well.

This is rare in today's culture of constant migration. We lack permanence and the sense of a home place. With this detachment, our culture is developing a tacit assumption that family relationships are optional and family heritage is irrelevant. But I digress.

A good way to understand life in Dunnavant is to hear the story of one who visited often as a child.

Story Five

Dunnavant Relived

Edna Horning's childhood home was Gadsden, Alabama, but she began visiting her Dunnavant grandparents, Mr. and Mrs. Edward Holladay, in infancy. She continued through her formative years into early adulthood. The story that follows are her memories of Dunnavant from the 1950-60s period.

In my early childhood, the only warmth [at my Grandparents' house] was provided by a wood-burning fireplace in the living room and two coal-burning stoves, one in the front bedroom and other in the kitchen. After a hod of bituminous, also known as a bloody big bucket of rocks, was brought in by someone grunting and sweating a lot, Grandmother or Granddaddy would open the topside by a loosely attached handle of coiled metal and tip in as many lumps as needed. Seeing the orange flames roaring away inside like something from the earth's core always unnerved me, and I usually averted my eyes after a few seconds.

The old-fashioned cast iron stove in the kitchen, with its heavy lids requiring the use of lid lifters, was of the type that could have been (and in the past probably had been) used for cooking, although that function had already been appropriated by the modern stove I knew. Its sole remaining purpose was to warm the kitchen, which it did exceedingly well. Sleepers who drew the back bedroom during the frigid months were privileged to comfort their feet against a brick that Grandmother would heat in the fireplace, wrap heavily in newspaper, and then shove under the covers. At first it felt oh-so-good but by morning had become as cold as, well, as a brick in winter. The one and only bathroom had a plug-in space heater.

In the living room to the left of the fireplace was a feature which must have been commonplace in its day but which I have never seen elsewhere before or since: a sturdy, rectangular window seat which doubled as a wood box accessible from outside as well as inside the house. Someone outside could life a hinged flap and push an armload of firewood into the enclosure. Someone inside merely had to lift the top of the window seat to remove the logs as needed. Over time its function as a wood box became impractical, fading away as more and more books and magazines were piled on it. I would curl up there for hours, my favorite place to read or do homework.

When I was still small enough to fit inside, I bathed at least a few times in one of those galvanized tubs firmly fixed in images of country life. Should the hot water prove unequal to increased demands, water had to be simmered on the stoves in pots and then transferred wherever. Vigilance as well as patience was advisable for such undertakings because hot water theft, I deeply regret to report, had been known to occur should the waiting person step out of the kitchen.

Eventually the coal burners were replaced by gas heaters and the handheld kerosene lanterns by flashlights, but until then we were contentedly living in a firetrap. A thousand wonders we didn't all burn to death.

A large part of Dunnavant's appeal was that Bruce (my younger brother) and I could, as Mother once put it, "take over the place," by which she meant we could charge around and explore the homestead and adjacent territories with abandon. Though my grandparents were not farmers as such, they owned no animals themselves, they sometimes allowed neighbors and acquaintances to use their land and buildings for sundry agricultural purposes. I remember stroking a tethered cow grazing in the pasture. I recall bouncing around in a corn crib half full of old, dried out cobs and shucks until I saw a glistening black snake patiently waiting on a nearby ledge to feast on mice that also came in. I immediately decided to play elsewhere.

I watched chickens nest in broody boxes nailed to one side of the barn and was delighted whenever one rose to reveal a smooth, creamy egg underneath. I once saw a chicken have its neck wrung and the frightening way it flopped about after the deed was done.

When very young, I queried a local woman who kept chickens why she bothered to have a rooster in the flock. I knew that hens laid eggs and were, therefore, good for something, but roosters? They did not do anything and hence were utterly useless, as far as I could tell. Her explanations, none too specific, did not clear up the mystery. City children may derive pleasure from the country's day-to-day charms but do not necessarily draw correct conclusions about its day-to-day workings.

Granddaddy kept a grape arbor and Grandmother tended a strawberry patch, daffodils, hollyhocks, four-o'clocks, verbena, and blooming shrubbery, and maintained an apple and pear orchard behind the house. She made pickled peaches, which I never liked, and the tastiest country fried steak in the county, which everyone liked. With advancing age these and other activities were discontinued one by one. But the two of them, Granddaddy in particular, were to remain ambulatory until the very end of their lives, and no doubt the exertion necessary for these and other activities were partially responsible.

In springtime, Grandaddy would lift us up to see nests the birds had made on the branches and the newly hatched babies inside, and in fall we gathered the fruit from the ground and the low-hanging limbs. One October, he walked us up the road to a Halloween carnival at the schoolhouse—just one large room with an interior capable of being closed off into smaller spaces—that Mother and Aunt Camma had attended as children. It was there I experienced cakewalks, bobbing for apples, and the carving of jack-o'-lanterns for the first time.

One chilly afternoon, Bruce and I flew kites on a parcel of cleared land behind the orchard, and the event is still enshrined in my memory as the only successful kite-flying attempt of my life. All other tries, before or after, were duds. Bruce's kite was bright green and mine blue, and until evening fell we remained fixed like statues, delighted by our accomplishment and by the lozenge-shaped wonders suspended against the darkening sky.

The chances that we had brought the kites with us from Gadsden I adjudge slim. It is more likely that they were purchased at Bowdoin's Store, which deserves, at the very least, an entire chapter unto itself in the Dunnavant archives. Situated at the intersection of Highway 25 and the unpaved road leading to the house, it was, as the crow flies, no more than a thousand feet away, but actual walking distance was greater since the dirt trail there and back traversed the side of a moderately steep gully. At the nadir of the gully was a small stream running perpendicular to the road and sometimes snakes could be seen sunning themselves on the sandy banks.

If Grandmother escorted us there once, I don't remember it. It was invariably Granddaddy who said, "Let's go to Bowdoin's!" and the three of us would set off on foot. On average, a one-way trip probably took no more than ten minutes but seemed longer to children eager for treats. It's amazing to me, considering the numerous times Bruce and I were taken there, that I can't picture exactly what Bowdoin's sold. We were focused exclusively on the candy, drinks, and small toys available and paid scant attention to other details. I feel certain that more substantial items such as groceries, batteries, etc. were also available but cannot say for sure. Small though it was, Bowdoin's did not lack for business, and many depended on it. Even today, long after its demise, area residents still refer to the building as Bowdoin's Store and use it as a landmark when giving directions.

Since before I was born, Grandmother had been the postmistress for the Dunnavant community and was just coming to the end of her working days when I was perhaps eight or nine. Her duties, which probably had never required more than a few hours a week were performed in "the post office." It was situated perhaps a hundred feet from the house. Mail was terribly important to the local residents; they would silently gather in the evening, hopeful that something interesting or useful or informative might come that day from the outside world.

Because the mail was brought by a speeding freight that did not stop, the day's delivery had to be thrown off. When Bruce and I were there, we watched the train come around the bend, its whistle screaming at eardrum-piercing level, until an open box car passed and a heavy-duty canvas sack was tossed out the door. As soon as the train was quite gone, and not a second before, we were allowed to run to the side of the rails, retrieve the sack, and with an air of great importance carry it to the post office. Grandmother would unbuckle a stout leather strap at the open end and shake onto the table whatever was inside. Sometimes there was much, sometimes a single item, but either way she dutifully proceeded to postmark each one with a hand stamp and place them in their proper slots.

    Receiving is generally easier than giving, as it is in life, and so it was with the outgoing mail. More effort was required. The previous day's delivery sack had to be filled, bound, and then carried to a specially designed pole where it was suspended like a hanged felon. As the train passed, someone inside yet another open box car reached out with a specially designed pole and hooked the sack with lightning speed. Snap. Gone. Now you saw it, now you didn't.

    Occasionally, however, the train was obliged to come to a complete halt. Now and again someone would order, for example, a shipment of baby chicks and such cargo could hardly be thrown off a moving train. They would arrive in a flat box barely tall enough to allow the cheeping biddies to stand upright. Fascinated, I would put a finger in the air holes and stroke the soft yellow down on the tiny heads.

    The letters that I and others had sent over time never required an address more finite than Mr. and Mrs. E. D. Holladay, Dunnavant, Alabama. Nothing so labeled ever failed to get where it was going, and not just because my grandmother was postmistress; the same principle held true for everyone else. Even zip codes were still a year or two off. Dunnavant seemed blissfully timeless. But circa 1959, two changes occurred. The first meant little to us children, but the second presaged much darker matters. The terse mailing address for my grandparents was officially lengthened to Box 378-T, Route 1, Leeds. And the county, invoking eminent domain, put a paved road right through the center of our property.

The new road, essentially an extension of Highway 41, split twenty-four of the prettiest contiguous acres you ever laid eyes on into seventeen on one side and seven on the other. The barns, corncrib, tool shed, strawberry patch, flower beds, and rock wall, being in the very midst, were bulldozed into oblivion. Even a twelve-year-old could grasp that did not bode well.

And it didn't. Mother used to say afterwards that that road killed Grandmother, and she may have been right. Evidently, Grandmother was never reconciled to it, and the distress began to affect her health.

The Dunnavant chapter in our lives would soon draw to a close. Grandmother succumbed to a series of strokes on February 12, 1963, her 80th birthday. After returning to Dunnavant where he lived alone for perhaps another twelve months, Granddaddy was obliged by advancing feebleness to make his home alternately with us and with Aunt Camma.

Thereafter, excepting brief trips to retrieve various items or check on something, Dunnavant faded into the shadows while Bruce and I moved into a future occupied with college and graduate school and self-support. Granddaddy was to die in July of 1973 at age 96.

Author's note: This account is excerpted from Ms. Horning's excellent paper entitled "Dunavant Redivivus." (Redivivus means relived or restored.) A hardcopy of Ms. Horning's paper is located at the Shelby County Historical Society.

Ms. Horning recalls the spelling of her grandparents' community as "Dunavant" rather than the spelling prominent today of "Dunnavant." The spelling was changed in the excerpt above for clarity.

Story Six

The Winding Stair Trail

In his 1933 novel *Lost Horizon*, author James Hilton describes a hidden valley in the Himalayas with mystical qualities. The Dunnavant Valley has its own mystique especially when clouds conceal the ridge tops. Descending into the valley on Hugh Daniel Drive prompts a feeling of a remote place, far removed from the busy commercial corridor one just left behind.

Many claim that in summer the Dunnavant Valley is several degrees cooler than the 280 corridor. The elevation increase between Hugh Daniel at Highway 280, and Hugh Daniel at Dunnavant Valley Road, net of the mountain crossing, is only about 200 feet. This is hardly a climate game changer. No polar bears are headed our way.

But in my humble opinion, and I think James Spann will back me on this, the tree-canopied peace of the Dunnavant Valley is bound to be several *mental* degrees cooler than an eight-lane heatsink full of fumes and feral traffic. Just a guess mind you.

Because of the rugged ridgelines, Dunnavant Valley has only a limited number of primary access roads: congested Highway 280 to the south, Hugh Daniel Drive in the middle, and Highway 25 in the north. The rich history behind Highway 280, historically known as the Florida Short Route, has already been discussed. But there is also a story behind Highway 25 involving a little known community called Calcis, located eleven miles south of Dunnavant.

Calcis is named after the calcium found in the limestone under its soil. Limestone is an essential constituent in steel making: central Alabama is one of the few locations where all three ingredients of steel-making—iron ore, coal and limestone—are found in close proximity. During the iron and steel age of Alabama, limestone was quarried in Calcis and sent through the Dunnavant Valley railroad tunnels to the thundering blast furnaces in Birmingham.

Calcis was the location of a 3,000 acre camp belonging to Sidney Word Lee. Mr. Lee (1864-1944) founded the Buffalo Rock Company and he did quite well selling ginger ale. Lee claimed Calcis was the most beautiful area in the world and through Lee's encouragement (and money) a road was built from Calcis over Double Oak Mountain.[1]

Although the exact route is lost to time, Mr. Lee's road probably employed what is shown on the 1908 USGS map as Wyatts Gap.[2] Construction began in 1914 but because of the rugged terrain took seven years to complete. The curves, switchbacks, and inclines must have been dramatic because the locals nicknamed it the "Winding Stair Trail." If the topography of Highway 25 is any indication, today's drivers will agree it was aptly named.

In 1930, the Alabama highway department completed Highway 21 as an "unimproved" road connecting Leeds through Dunnavant to Calcis.[3]

Like Edna Horning in Dunnavant, I spent much time as a youngster in the country with my grandparents. In rural Tennessee, as in Alabama, the roads were chert, a chalky yellow gravel. With chert roads, the first thing to notice was the corrugations or "wash-boarding" at curves and corners. The chert formed rock-hard wavelets that would vibrate automobile passengers like a paint-shaker at Lowes. This was especially true when Dad had the "pedal to the metal."

But other than minor brain damage, the primary problem with chert roads was the dust billowing for the length of a football field behind the station wagon (an early form of SUV). It caked roadside vegetation and the back windshield of a car like yellow icing. Rear visibility was quite impossible, but was unnecessary. At my Dad's speed, nobody was going to catch us from the rear.

When approaching oncoming traffic, both cars frantically rolled-up the windows. (Electric windows? Nope. AC in a car? Nope.) Without quick reflexes, the passengers would be blinded, choked, and covered in yellow powder when the following cloud of dust caught-up and swallowed the vehicle. Both drivers slowed and gingerly found a wide spot in the narrow road to pass. With the side mirrors tapping (if so equipped), the cars or pickups slipped by each other. A courtesy wave to the other vehicle was absolutely mandatory by rural etiquette.

Once passed, ludicrous speed was resumed.

Overjoyed with a road regardless of its surfacing, the towns of Leeds, Dunnavant, Vandiver, Sterrett, and Calcis were linked to Vincent and Harpersville by a state-maintained road. The road begun by Mr. Lee connected the Coosa River Valley with the Cahaba River Valley. The pioneers laboriously trekking along the river valleys to enter Shelby County could never have imagined this day.

In 1955, thirty-seven long years after it was opened, Highway 21 was paved from Leeds to Harpersville.[4] Two years later, it was re-designated as the Highway 25 we know today.[5] Drivers may not know it, but the Double Oak Mountain section of Highway 25 crosses over the railroad tunnel bored through the core of the mountain twice, both driving up to and down from Wyatts Gap.

The Scenic Drive

Today, the smooth paved roadway of Highway 25 from Leeds to Harpersville winds its way through picturesque country: mountaintop views of forest covered hills and valleys, verdant pastures, and deep woodlands largely untouched by development. Shelby County is truly beautiful: this is one of many scenic, unspoiled drives through the county.

On your way, stop in Sterrett for an RC and a MoonPie. Be careful to share the road with motorcycles and bicyclers. Time your drive to be at the craggy lookout on Wyatts Gap at sunset; you will discover an inspirational view of Dunnavant Valley below.

Story Seven

By the Light of the Moon

Moonshine is named after the "lesser light that governs the night." However, nocturnal brewing was not prompted by the romance of a moonlit evening. It had everything to do with avoiding revenuers, known within the moonshiner community as "revenooers."

Revenuers were law enforcement agents who collected excise taxes and jailed unlicensed distillers. They were about as popular as rattlesnakes on a rabbit ranch. President Washington became the first revenuer when he put down the "Whiskey Rebellion" of Pennsylvania distillers. These early moonshiners thought taxing liquor was against their rights. Bless their hearts.

A nationwide temperance movement to ban alcoholic beverages was active even before the Civil War. By 1874, twenty-two Alabama counties had voted to go "dry." In a November 1907 special session, the Alabama legislature decided to go whole hog: it adopted statewide prohibition of the production and distribution of alcoholic beverages. The *Shelby County Sun* proudly proclaimed on September 17, 1914:

> . . . Shelby is a prohibition county. The citizens are sober. But this was not so always. There was a time when some of its citizens took a nip for the stomach's sake. This is evident in the fact that on the old ordinance books of the county still in the vaults, there is a law regulating the price to be charged for a drink of whiskey. This was back in the days when Alabama was a territory.[1]

But methinks the proclamation of sobriety was premature.

The Eighteenth Amendment to the United States Constitution, which prohibited intoxicating liquors across the nation, was on the books from 1919 through 1933. Since it was already dry, Alabama's illicit alcohol production was probably way ahead of the nation even before the national ban. Prohibition, however, took the production of the "liquid crop" to a whole 'nother level.

On December 20, 1928, at the peak of nationwide prohibition, the *Shelby County Reporter* related:

> Wholesale prices for corn brewed whisky in Shelby County increased approximately 100 percent in the past month after actions of federal prohibition agents . . . During that period 66 moonshine outfits were put out of business by the agents, who poured out between 30,000 and 40,000 gallons of corn mash . . .[2]

The *Shelby County Reporter* article went on to say, "During the period of seven weeks, when the dry officers made trips back, many stills were found erected, new, or under construction on the same sites where others were destroyed three days before."

It would seem that a decade after the *Shelby County Sun's* teetotaling assertion, some citizens had not just fallen off the wagon, but had pushed it into the Cahaba River.

For Shelby County moonshiners, also known as bootleggers, the prime market was the rapidly growing city of Birmingham. The *Shelby County Reporter* article referenced above, stated that Birmingham's Jefferson County was one of the largest buyers of Shelby County moonshine.

Moonshiners hid their little factories, or "stills," deep in the hollows of the hills and ridges of north Shelby County. Some stills even had multiple flues that dispersed the smoke to avoid detection. The area now known as Oak Mountain State Park was a hiding place for many stills.

The primary ingredients of moonshine spirits are yeast, corn and sugar. The moonshiners were typically farmers who grew their own corn but bought the sugar at their local general store. Moonshiners spread their purchases to multiple stores, lest they tip off government agents by their lopsided sugar consumption. Some stores had a problem with moonshiners robbing their sugar supply.

The Narrows was a prime location for moonshiners who needed isolation and good water. One local resident reported he could stand on his front porch and count the smoke from eight different stills at one time.[3]

When the Florida Short Route was completed, the highway between Chelsea and Jefferson County attracted lively entertainment and even a gambling casino. Establishments mentioned in the *Shelby County Reporter* include the Narrows Inn and the Forest Inn.[4]

The *Shelby County Reporter* described an eye witness account of the robbery of a casino in The Narrows. The witness said:

> "I was doorman, and here come a bunch of stick-up men—seven of 'em. They saw me fumbling for my gun and kicked the door in. When they lined all the men up against the wall, a couple fellers couldn't get their hands up high enough!
>
> "One guy ran and hid all his money in the coal by the furnace in the basement. When he came up he had black soot all over his white shirt. I started laughing and one of the stickup men hit me and said what was so funny.
>
> "When they left, we all needed some nerve medicine. I had some store-bought whiskey hid on the front porch and we all had some."[5]

In the moonshiners' defense, farming was a hardscrabble occupation in the first half of the 1900s, particularly during the Great Depression years. Often, men would follow logging operations, sharecrop, or work whatever menial jobs they could find to feed their families. The temptation to live outside the law must have been strong.

In the December 10, 1981, issue of the *Shelby County Reporter,* a Chelsea resident highlighted the dire predicament many faced:

> "There wasn't nothing much a fellow could do to make money then, I used to walk six miles to the sawmill, work ten hours, and

only make 50 cents. I started figuring it up one morning and I was walking 72 miles a week and making $3.00. I couldn't pay my bill to the commissary.

"I told the man (at the mill) this was my last day. He said what are you going to do, and I said I was going to make whiskey. You could sell whiskey for a dollar a gallon, and wasn't long before I had an old Studebaker '6' and was driving it to the still."[6]

Making moonshine became an archaic way of life when Shelby County voted to legalize alcoholic sales in the 1970s.

If you hike along the base of the mountains in Dunnavant Valley, you might stumble across the crumbling stone chimney of a former still. It's all that's left of the once thriving cottage industry pursued by the light of the moon.

Author's note: Appreciation for information goes to Liz Clayton, contributor to Shelby County History & Heritage, *and Virginia Randolph, longtime Dunnavant Valley resident.*

And also to the Shelby County Reporter *for its in-depth reporting of events which becomes the history we look back on today.*

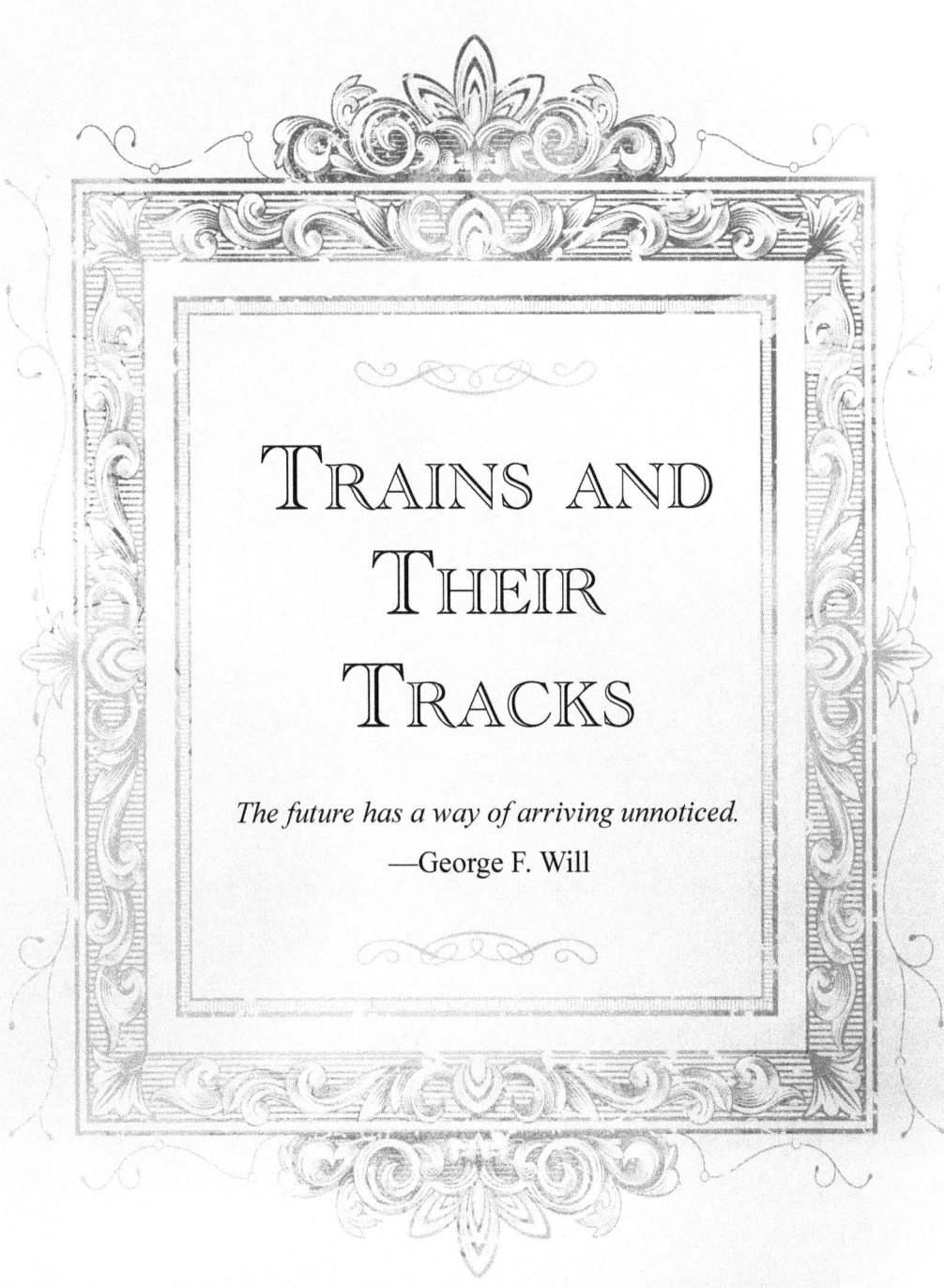

Trains and Their Tracks

The future has a way of arriving unnoticed.
—George F. Will

Story Eight

Highways of Iron

On January 29, 1886, Carl Benz applied for a patent for his "vehicle powered by a gas engine." The patent—number 37435—may be regarded as the birth certificate of the automobile.[1]

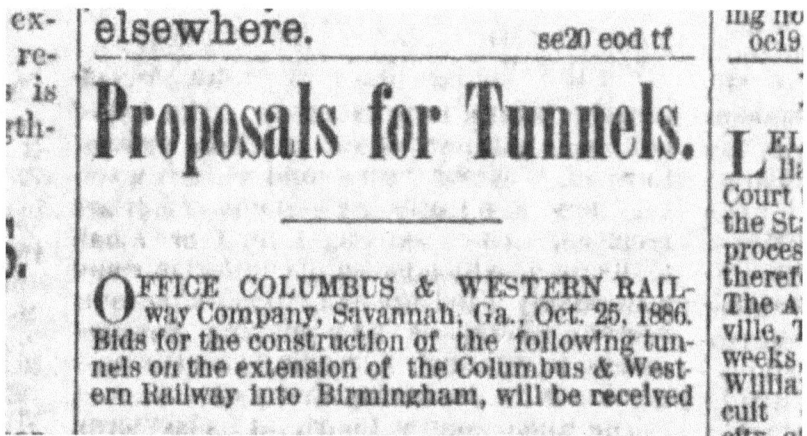

Automobile ownership is a prerequisite for sentient life in the US today. Almost everyone in Alabama with a driver's license and a pulse has a car, or so every teenager tells their parents. It's a good bet that the population of automobiles in the Dunnavant Valley is 'purt near equal to the number of adults.

But envision the days past when the SUV, the pickup, and the "crossover" did not exist—were not even imagined. Consequently, there were no gas stations and no stoplights. Few, if any, of the valley's roads were paved. Depending on the season, a dusty or muddy wagon track would be the only way to your house.

If your mind's eye can capture that life, you have some idea why railroads dominated long-distance travel. In the 1800s, to get anywhere inland required a horse, a river, or a train. Railroads were the de facto interstate highways.

Given the scarcity of roads, and in the absence of waterways, towns tended to spring up along railroads. The Columbus and Western Railway began operations through the north end of the Shoal Creek Valley (now known as Dunnavant Valley) in 1888 and Dunnavant appears on the 1892 USGS map. Chelsea was formed in 1908 when the Atlanta, Birmingham and Atlantic Railway was laid. It's a noteworthy historical fact that Dunnavant made it on the map sixteen years before Chelsea.

The first railroad in Alabama consisted of two miles of track near Tuscumbia in 1830. This horse-drawn short line of the Tuscumbia Railway enabled cotton being transported down the Tennessee River by barge to be efficiently carted around the shoals in the river. During the "golden age" of railroads, from the time of the Civil War to the 1920s, a building boom resulted in a peak of 5,000 miles of rail lines crisscrossing Alabama.

Dunnavant Valley's two railroad tunnels are a little-known testament to the boom-time of railroading. The tunnel projects were put out for bids from prospective contractors in October 1886. An ad in a Nashville newspaper, *The Daily American*, placed by the Columbus and Western Railway, described the tunnels:

> COOSA TUNNEL, about 2,400 feet long, five or six miles southeast of Leeds' Station, on the Georgia Pacific Railroad.
>
> OAK MOUNTAIN TUNNEL, about 1,150 feet long, two or three miles southeast of Leeds'.[2]

Both tunnels were to be completed by August 15, 1887. On June 21, 1888, the *Weekly Iron Age* recorded the rail line completion:

> Yesterday was a memorable day in the history of the Columbus and Western Railway [later Central of Georgia, and today Norfolk Southern]. The last spike on the extension of this road, from Goodwater to Birmingham, was driven near Coosa Mountain Tunnel [Double Oak Mountain Tunnel], in Shelby County.[3]

The two Dunnavant Valley railroad tunnels are still in regular service, as the late-night moaning of locomotives attest.

Today, even after fierce competition from truck and automobile, some 3,000 miles of railway are located in Alabama compared to 1,130 miles of interstate highway. Bulk shipment of new automobiles employs enclosed rail cars called "autoracks." New cars are distributed by semi-truck from rail terminals.

What a modern paradox: Steel wheels gotta turn before the rubber hits the road.

Double Oak Mountain Tunnel (or Coosa Tunnel)
Norfolk Southern Railway *(Courtesy Charles Wright)*

Story Nine

John Henry's Race

John Henry kissed his hammer; kissed it with a groan. Sighed a sigh and closed his weary eyes.

—The legend of John Henry, Steel Driving Man (origin unknown)

The Minnesota legend of Paul Bunyan and Babe, his blue ox, says the pair competed in a tree felling competition with a steam-powered chainsaw. Folklore says Bunyan and Babe lost to the newfangled device.

Dunnavant has a claim to a similar story related to the railroad tunnel through Oak Mountain, just a few miles south of Leeds, Alabama. It involves the legendary John Henry, the steel driving man. But unlike the Bunyan tale, John Henry triumphs.

John Henry's story, sometimes spelled Jawn Henry, has a long oral history. It was first recorded as a ballad in a songbook by author Guy Johnson in 1929. Since then, the story has captivated musicians for nearly a century. It has been recorded in various arrangements by Harry Belafonte, Van Morrison, Woodie Guthrie, Bruce Springsteen, and Johnny Cash.[1] Growing up, I was only aware of the Tennessee Ernie Ford rendition; I'd have gladly accepted any of the others over Ernie's.

A number of locations compete for the honor of being the actual historical site behind the legend. At one time or another, John Henry was said to have died in ten different states plus Jamaica. I'm sure all have interesting justifications, but in this story we will concentrate on two leading contenders: the Columbus and Western Railway's Oak Mountain Tunnel in the Dunnavant Valley, and the Lewis Tunnel of the Chesapeake and Ohio Railway in Virginia.

The tunnel construction method of the period was to drive a long steel drill shaft into the rock, by hand, with hammer blows. The man holding the drill was the "shaker." This role got its name because the shaker had to frequently turn the drill and shake out the rock debris. The man striking the drill with a sledge hammer was the "steel driver." Once the drill was driven the requisite distance into the rock—ten feet or more, the hole was filled with dynamite and detonated. The broken rock was then cleared away and the process was repeated.

The Oak Mountain version of the story has been researched by Professor John Garst of the University of Georgia.[2] In the professor's well-founded opinion, John Henry Dabney was a former slave from Copiah County, Mississippi. He worked in the construction crew of the chief engineer for the Columbus and Western Railway. John Henry was a steel-driver and from all accounts must have been a uniquely powerful and talented man.

His existence is documented by the 1870 census for Copiah County, Mississippi, which lists a John Henry Dabney, twenty years old and married.

The Oak Mountain and Double Oak Mountain tunnels were bored through the mountains in 1887. According to Garst's research, the salesman of a steam-powered drill pitched his device to the chief engineer, John Henry's boss. The engineer was skeptical so a competition was proposed. John Henry agreed to compete with the machine for a prize if he won. A huge crowd came to watch the battle which took place at the east portal of the Oak Mountain Tunnel (which is in Dunnavant Valley) on September 20, 1887.

Man and machine set to it. One version says John Henry used a hammer in each hand to pound away at the drill shaft. Finally, time was called, the white dust settled, and the echoes of steel clanging on steel faded away. The depth of the steam-powered drill measured nine feet, but John Henry's drill was driven into the solid rock to a depth of fourteen feet!

Man beat machine. However, the story has a poignant ending. John Henry fainted at the end of the contest. He regained consciousness briefly and called for his wife. He told her he was blind and weak, symptoms of a heart rupture. John Henry asked her if he "had beat that old steam drill." She assured him he had, and with that contentment, he passed away with his head cradled in her lap.

Edna Horning, in her circa 1950 Dunnavant memory, adds a local confirmation:

> . . . David and Bruce [Edna's cousin and brother] spent hours searching the mountain-side in hope of finding the final resting place of John Henry, the legendary "Steel Driving Man" who had been born a slave and, according to strong and apparently reliable and documented local tradition, was buried in Dunnavant, the exact location of the grave having been lost over time. Only recently did I know that Granddaddy, born in 1877, had actually been acquainted with John Henry although the two men were at least three decades apart in age.

The view of Professor Garst is very convincing and Ms. Horning's testimony provides a final blow (excuse the pun) to alternate stories. Garst believes John Henry Dabney is buried just outside the Sand Ridge Cemetery. This location is slightly less than two miles as the crow flies from the Oak Mountain tunnel. Another source believes he was buried outside the work camp which would probably have been near the tunnel.

The Opposing Side

A William & Mary University professor issued a rebuttal to Professor Garst (included in the Garst article referenced above). His case suggests John Henry was one John William Henry—a convict from Old Virginia Penitentiary—who was allotted to work on the Chesapeake and Ohio (C&O) rail line. The race with the steam drill would have happened sometime in 1868-72 when the C&O's Lewis Tunnel was constructed.

Well, right off the name is wrong. Next, the professor says his John William was 5' 1" tall, hardly the size one would expect for a steel driving man. Finally, in this version the steel driver died of a stroke, but a stroke wouldn't produce John Henry's symptoms.

In still another version, the National Park Service (NPS) has John Henry's triumph at an additional disputed location: the C&O Railway tunnel known as Big Bend in Talcott, West Virginia.³ The NPS has erected an eight foot bronze statue of "John Henry" at this location. Your tax dollars were put to faulty work: a government statue doesn't decide history.

An article in the *Central of Georgia Railway Magazine*, October 1930 (framed on the wall in the Leeds, Alabama, railroad depot), claims John Henry raced steam drills at both Big Bend and Oak Mountain. However, the article says it was the Oak Mountain Tunnel in Dunnavant Valley where he met his demise.

The City of Leeds has all the proof it needs. An official proclamation, dated September 18, 2006, declares that "this icon and hero" be honored on the third weekend of September with a John Henry Day.

Conclusion

Technology is created by humans, but it tends to de-humanize its creator. We all love our wonderful devices, yet at times they make the good qualities of humanity superfluous. John Henry's story highlights the dignity of human labor when contrasted with a machine. This is why the drama of John Henry has endured and been celebrated by so many artists in so many mediums.

Vulcan has long needed a brother. I would propose to the good folk of Dunnavant Valley that we band together and place a muscular statue of John Henry at the intersection of Dunnavant Valley Road and Highway 25. Ten feet tall in Birmingham's native cast iron should about do it (not some wimpy bronze). Close by should be a plaque with Professor Garst's account of this classic tale.

Who knows, the University of Georgia might make a contribution to honor Alabama's folklore. Or not.

Story Ten

Sounds of the Valley

In the classic film *It's a Wonderful Life*, George Bailey named his three favorite sounds: anchor chains, plane motors, and train whistles. Dunnavant Valley accommodates the sounds of trains from the two major railroads that bookend the valley. To the southwest, the CSX Transportation rail line runs under County Road 280 (formerly two-lane Highway 280). At the northeast end of the valley, running through Dunnavant and parallel to Highway 25, is the Norfolk Southern rail line.

The track through Dunnavant with its two tunnels was originally built by the Columbus and Western Railway. This company was organized in 1880 to connect Columbus, Georgia, with Birmingham; the Dunnavant segment of its railroad was put into operation in 1888. Just seven years later in 1895, after a convoluted series of mergers, the line was taken over by the Central of Georgia Railway. The Central of Georgia enjoyed sixty-eight years of stability, and then was purchased by the Southern Railway in 1963, which subsequently became part of Norfolk Southern Railway in 1982.[1]

The Norfolk Southern line has four grade crossings within the valley in the space of one and a half miles—three county roads and one state highway. The most likely reverberations we hear in the valley are the warning blasts from the locomotive's air horns as the railway's trains approach one of these road crossings.

The Federal Department of Transportation website commands, "Train horns must be sounded in a standardized pattern of two long, one short and one long blasts."[2] The DOT website goes on to say that the engineer must start blowing the horn between fifteen to twenty seconds before reaching the crossing and continue until the lead locomotive occupies the crossing. The horn volume is between 90 and 110 decibels, which is equivalent to a commercial jet plane revving up to take-off speed. It isn't a warning that can be easily missed, which is the intent.

Any doubts as to why all the horn blowing is necessary? Think of that final scene in the *Back to the Future III* movie when a train obliterates Doc Brown's DeLorean time machine.

Besides air horns, it's also possible to hear the throbbing of the locomotive's diesel engines. At an elevation of 800 feet, the Oak Mountain tunnel is the high point between Leeds and Dunnavant Valley. So, going toward Leeds, the engines strain to pull their load up the grade from the Coosa Mountain tunnel to the Oak Mountain tunnel. And in the opposite direction, even after the locomotive has passed thru the Oak Mountain tunnel into the valley, it's still pulling the mile or so of train behind it up the grade from Leeds.

In this twist of topography, depending somewhat on the length of the train, a locomotive passing through Dunnavant Valley is always pulling a load up the grade to the Oak Mountain tunnel. A diesel-electric locomotive is comparable to 3,000 horses, and usually two or more are ganged together. A herd of that size creates quite a rumbling. Remember the stampede scene in the movie *Australia*.

Why are the sounds more apparent at night? It's a matter of timing and physics. At night, there's less competition from daytime sounds like construction and road traffic. Also at night, a temperature inversion can occur in the valley, meaning cooler air is capped with warmer air above. Because the speed of sound goes up as air temperature goes down, an inversion has the effect of reflecting the sound further down the valley. With the right temperature and wind direction, trains can be heard eight miles away.

The mournful sound of locomotive horns and the low rumbling of their engines can be heard almost the entire length of our valley. These iconic sounds compete with crickets and tree frogs to add personality to the still, quiet evenings of the Dunnavant Valley.

INTERLUDE

*Do not move an ancient boundary stone
or encroach on the fields of the fatherless,
for their Defender is strong.*
—Proverbs 23:10-11

Story Eleven

Past Yet Present

Author's note: The following excerpts are from the article "Shelby County History" by Frances Saiia as printed in the Shelby County Advertiser, *June 6, 1974.*

These fifty-year-old comments seem prophetic of our current time.

Shelby County has, within a span of a century and a half, run the gamut, from the crude, rugged pioneer to the pampered, affluent planter; from the pitifully half-starved product of the Depression years, up to the new breed of the present era: the no-nonsense, hard-driving business executive.

The county is today divided into two factions. The surge of growth from the neighboring Jefferson County on the north has brought with it a new breed of people. For the most part, they are well-educated and sophisticated—the typical upper middle class suburbanite. They come to Shelby County wanting all the good things the suburban dweller takes for granted: water, sewer, proper sanitation service, a proper plan for growth, good schools, etc.

Meanwhile, the native, a descendent of the county's earliest settler, bitterly resents this invasion of new people, who bring with them new ideas, and clamor for new laws—laws which threaten to disrupt his present lifestyle. His heretofore predictable future is no longer so predictable. Changes are coming too fast. He is angry and bewildered. He feels he's being pushed about by powers over which he has no control.

The county officials, themselves pulled two ways, try in vain to bring the two factions to a point of understanding, meanwhile striving desperately to bring about order to what might soon very well be chaos.

An era is passing in Shelby County. The sleepy farming county is feeling the birth pangs of a new life.

It tries to close its ears to the roar of the bulldozer which rips into and mutilates the achingly beautiful pasture lands and wooded hillsides, making way for sleek, ultra-modern subdivisions, apartment complexes and shopping centers.

Life goes on very much as before for the county's southern-most residents, but in north Shelby County, it is increasingly hard to find a spot of land untouched or not just about to be touched by the hand of progress.

It's with mixed emotions that most of the citizens of the county greet this new era. The farsighted man says, "Let's make plans to control this on-coming growth while there's still time." The conservative says, "Let's wait and see. It may not be so bad." While the native, ever reluctant to change, stubbornly shakes his head and insists, "Never!"[1]

Life Between the Ridges

*There is a time for everything,
and a season for every activity under heaven.*
—Ecclesiastes 3:1

Story Twelve

Rodents and Rogues

The conflict started after our loyal Labrador, Tucker, retired from his post guarding our castle and went to dog heaven. The very next day, I heard scratching at the front door. Two bulging eyes and a twitching gray tail were hanging by tiny claws on the wooden sash of the front door. The creature was brazenly conducting an inventory of our living room through the glass. At my approach, a cheeky squirrel bounded away with maniacal chattering trailing behind.

Who initiated hostilities? I will testify on a pile of extermination manuals that it wasn't me. For my part, I could have enjoyed watching the little tree rats scamper across my yard. But let's enumerate the interlopers' atrocities: Who got in whose attic making a mess of whose insulation? Who ate through whose irrigation pipes, twice? Who chewed through whose Christmas lights in a brash act of bushy-tailed blasphemy?

Warming to a fight, I tried non-lethal deterrents. First, I applied various repellant oils to my lawn, which promised to send the vermin to my neighbors. (Sorry.) Instead, the aroma seemed to attract more gray legions. Next, I bought a squirrel trap, which proved to be no help. No bait, seed, or nut would lure the pint-sized pirates into that cage.

I was forced to escalate the fight after an attack which let me know this was mortal combat. It was an ordinary work day as I pulled out on Highway 280 headed downtown. I was negotiating through the normal rush hour road rage, when my eye happened to catch my gas gauge: it was down a quarter of a tank. I thought to myself, *Didn't I fill up yesterday?* By The Summit, I was missing half a tank. In Homewood, the low fuel light came on and I stopped to refill. I drove straight to the company garage, then walked to work.

About an hour later, the mechanic called and said, "Mister, you should go buy a lottery ticket 'cause today is your lucky day. Something gnawed a hole in your fuel injector line. Gas is everywhere. You coulda caught fire!"

This was war and I was unarmed. I consulted Amazon and bought a scope-equipped pellet gun.

The hunt began. I figured out the best ammunition—and how to hide till the squirrels were in range. Without going into gory details, let's just say the score began to even up.

Squirrels are territorial, so it occurred to me that the fuel-line attack could be due to one particular rogue squirrel with an affinity for warm engines. This seemed confirmed the day I opened the hood of my wife's car and there, spread-eagled on the battery, was a charred gray body and the frayed remains of a bushy tail. I found tiny teeth marks on the red plastic cap of the positive terminal. All it took was a nose on the positive post, and a tail twitch to the metal hood, and zap—off to oblivion went my odious opponent.

The battle goes on, but the damage has subsided, perhaps due to my marksmanship, or perhaps to the insurgent's electrocution. The moral here for rogues? Don't poke your nose where it doesn't belong, and keep your tail to yourself.

Good advice for all God's creatures.

Story Thirteen

Dunnavant Redux

The demise of small town America is a familiar story. Like the forgotten Radiator Springs in the movie *Cars*, its melancholy tune resonates across rural America.

Road traffic eventually beat out the passenger service of the railroad, and trains no longer stopped in Dunnavant. Likewise, the post office found it more economic to operate the mail service from Leeds and the Dunnavant post office was closed. The old post office building was moved to another location to be preserved as a museum, but it burned.

By 1961, only Bowdoin's store and the Dunnavant Elementary School remained to mark the community.

> In 1970, my family moved to Roanoke, Alabama, population 5,251. The train depot had long been boarded up, but the storefronts along Main Street, in what was quaintly called "downtown," were vibrant. Two drugstores, two large hardware stores, a feed store, two groceries, an auto parts store, a movie theater, a jewelry store, a bank, City Café, and a Belk-Gallant department store were all doing well.
>
> Then Walmart opened two miles away on the "bypass." Within a decade, the stores of downtown were either gone or going.
>
> Today, only the feed store remains of the original businesses. Many of the roofs of the vacant stores eventually collapsed. The buildings were torn down leaving gaping holes in the storefronts like lanes in a forlorn bowling alley. Sure, there were other factors, but, to me, the precipitating element was the arrival of big-box marketing. America's "saving store" didn't save a town.

The School Burns

The average temperature on January 25, 1961 was 26 degrees in Birmingham. It was colder out in the country at Dunnavant. As so often happens, central Alabama had ice rather than snow. The roads over the ridgelines and in the valley itself were treacherous.

No one knows how the school fire started. Thankfully, it happened early, just before dawn. Otherwise, being a Wednesday, the three-room, wood-frame building would have been filled with the children and teachers who braved the winter weather.

The loss was complete: not a book, not a desk, not a lunchroom pot or pan was saved. Not even a piece of chalk. And not the new window curtains the students' mothers had just made.

One can imagine residents in the nearby homes, like the Holladays, rushing to the scene. The flames are roaring into the dark sky; glowing sparks swirl into the dim light of dawn. The heat stings their faces and the air smells of wood smoke. But all stood around helpless in the cold, and no doubt weeping, as the icon of a community burned to the ground.[1]

Dunnavant Elementary provided grades one through six in a common room format used since the earliest days of education. (My mother received her elementary education in a one-room school in rural Tennessee.) An article contributed to the *Heritage of Shelby County, Alabama* details the early history of education in Dunnavant (edited for clarity):

> The first school [in Dunnavant] was taught in a church, near what we called the "Headly Branch." Mr. J. O. Dorrough [Dorough?] was the teacher. Later the church was moved across the road in front of

what is now E. B. Bowdoin's Store. . . . Miss Blanche Head from Dadeville, Alabama, taught another group in a house located on the "J. H. Isbell place." Pleasant Ridge Church was the meeting place of still another group of students, and another also at Sand Ridge, making a total of four schools in Dunnavant Valley at one time. In 1922 and 1923, the schools were consolidated and the present schoolhouse was built. . . . There were many pleasant moments for young and old. Everyone worked in harmony to see that the building was equipped.[2]

It was this final building—in a long list of homes and churches used for schools—that burned in 1961.

The county education department arranged for the students to be bused to the Chelsea Elementary School at least for the interim. The parents appreciated the Chelsea reception of their students, but the daily thirty-five-mile round trip was a long haul for grade schoolers.

The PTA organized meetings with the county education superintendent. It was clear that the county had moved on from three-room schools; the current model was for larger central schools. And the number of students in Dunnavant was insufficient to build a full-size elementary. But the story does not end with young students on long bus rides.

The citizens of Dunnavant decided to rebuild their school. The PTA sold cakes and pies, hot lunches, and other merchandise. Fundraising plus donations brought in $6,000, and the county contributed the $5,000 it had received in insurance reimbursement. Not much by today's standards, but a great deal sixty years ago for a community of 100 families.

In May of 1962, construction started. Materials and furnishings were gifted to the school and work crews donated their time. The building was created block-by-block by the hands of the people. In August, the building was inspected, approved, and ready to receive students. When Shelby County schools opened on September 4, 1962, the brand new Dunnavant Elementary School welcomed eighty-three students. As a mother remarked to *The Birmingham News,* "The people here found out what it takes to get something you want that badly."[3]

The Firehouse

In 1989, the Dunnavant community organized and received certification for a volunteer fire company and the Dunnavant Volunteer Fire District (DVFD) was established. That was the easy part. They also needed a firehouse. Similar to the school rebuilding, fundraising efforts such as a turkey shoot brought in the needed funds. Materials and labor were donated and a supply of secondhand bricks was secured. The land for the facility, at the corner of Dunnavant Valley Road and Highway 25, was donated by a local family. The Shelby County Commission and the state forestry commission awarded money to buy equipment. It was all no small feat.

Today, the DVFD takes care of its own and coordinates with the fire departments of Leeds, Vandiver, and Cahaba Valley.

The DVFD faces unique contingencies because of the rail line running through its service area. At times, trains stop in Dunnavant Valley blocking one or more of the rail line's four road crossings. This becomes dangerous rather than inconvenient when the train blocks both legs of the loop created by County Road 41N and County Road 101 (also known as Mimosa Road). In this situation, the DVFD cannot cross the tracks from its main firehouse on Highway 25 and residents have no exit to get to medical services. For this contingency, the DVFD maintains firefighting equipment, at some expense, on both sides of the rail line.

A DVFD member related an emergency that occurred when the loop was blocked by a train. A small child had to be taken to a medical facility. The parents and members of the department passed the child by hand, in between the huge rail cars, over the coupling and brake lines, so as to get the child to a waiting vehicle on Highway 25.

Author's note: Trains blocking the Dunnavant road crossings for long periods is a longstanding danger for the affected residents. It has been repeatedly addressed with the railroad.

The Township

In 1993, in large measure to have control over the development that was creeping up the valley from Highway 280, a group of Dunnavant citizens circulated a petition to determine whether Dunnavant should become a township. One of the main reasons, according to a supporter, was to maintain the lifestyle of the residents.[4]

When the requisite number of signatures were secured, the Shelby County Probate Judge organized a special election for November 1993. The majority of the votes were favorable and The Town of Dunnavant was incorporated by order of the judge on January 14, 1994. Dunnavant was briefly Shelby County's newest municipality.

However, others in the community protested and a lawsuit was filed. The suit was successful and the election was overturned. In less than a year, the town limit signs were gathering dust in barns and basements.

Dunnavant has accomplished so much by pulling together. In the township question, it is intriguing to wonder whether both groups did not actually want the same thing: To be independent and free.

Story Fourteen

A Valentine Story

> There are three things that are too amazing for me,
> four that I do not understand:
> the way of an eagle in the sky,
> the way of a snake on a rock,
> the way of a ship on the high seas,
> and the way of a man with a maiden.
> —Proverbs 30:18-19

Men experienced with the daughters of Eve sneer at youthful Casanovas. Those new to "The Chase" brag that they know how to make the object of their affection happy on St. Valentine's Day. They believe women are knowable, but we men with Valentine purple hearts are not so easily deceived. We know that the rules of engagement can change as quickly as her smile when you offer flowers from Winn-Dixie.

The only constant in seeking the favor of a woman is the "Thought Factor." Somehow, in estrogen-speak, we communicate true love through our investment in creative energy. Men, take note! The Thought Factor is the pitiless female measurement by which ye shall be judged.

However, in a cruel twist of chromosomes, men are wired for the "Expediency Factor." We maximize our time for productive efforts, like watching multiple sporting events while trash-texting opposing buddies. Yeah, manly things like that.

Attempts to beat the Thought Factor may succeed once or twice with an uber-investment, like the ultimate enchilada—diamonds. But in the end, the Thought Factor trumps mere dollars. All who seek romance must enter therein.

My search for a Thought-Full Valentine gift commenced a week before while on a business trip. Of course, starting preparations on V-Day minus seven went against all of my Expediency genes, but walking through the airport, I came upon a kiosk stacked high with heart-shaped red-velvet candy boxes. Now candy—even chocolate—is a relatively worthless gift on the female Thought scale. It takes little creative energy. This purchase was just groundwork for the main event: the "Perfect Valentine Gift," also known among men as the PVG.

PVG Attempt #1. At her favorite department store on V-Day minus three, I took the long, dreaded ride on the up escalator to Ladies Wear. Reaching the top floor, I froze: before me was row after row and rack after rack of dresses and coats, along with things for the bottom half, somewhat like pants, and things for the top half, not shirts but still having arms and buttons. There were styles, colors, and patterns that made nuclear physics seem comprehensible by comparison. It was an alien moonscape. My palms began to sweat.

But aha! Just to my left was a chrome sign with a "Sale" placard. Now, I could understand a sale, and it was next to a table covered with, with . . . sweaters! Of course, it was cold outside. My imagination raced, contemplating her response: "Oh, how considerate of you to Think of me in this bitter cold weather!"

The only thing left to choose was color, and I learned color with crayons in first grade. Moments later, after sifting through 157 shades of red, I emerged from the destroyed sweater display triumphantly carrying the best PVG in the history of Western civilization. The sales clerk smiled as I approached, that condescending smirk reserved for men floundering in the ladies department. She coolly informed me that the sweater was not on sale—the chrome sign referred to the rack next to the table. The rack held a row of top-things stretching to Jupiter. I was a lost little boy.

I considered paying full price, but a man can only take so much embarrassment in Ladies Wear. I retreated on the down escalator licking my wounds.

PVG Attempt #2. Back on the first floor, I detected a safe alternative: jewelry. I circled the jewelry counter like a comet around the sun, not getting too close lest I melt. On my sixth or seventh orbit, the sales clerk asked if I needed assistance. Now, jewelry clerks are somehow less cynical than clothing clerks. Maybe it's because they are trapped within that island and befuddled men are a comic diversion.

The clerk pleasantly rattled through her well-worn list: a pearl necklace, a gold broach, gems from hard-to-pronounce African nations, birthstones . . . Wait, birthstone! It had a vaguely familiar feeling to it. I could get really creative and buy birthstone EAR-rings! Ha! I mused to myself, *What man has ever thought of this?* Seeing the gleam in the eye of her prey, the clerk praised my unsurpassed Thought-Fullness. Her use of the T-word clinched it. VISA did its magic and I smugly retired from the battlefield.

Daughters can be a decided asset with gifting guidance, so I called my college student to get confirmation of my brilliance. "What do you think of birthstone earrings for Mom?" I asked nonchalantly. She immediately replied, "Oh, Dad, are you brain-dead? You gave Mom that last year." I shifted into reverse to return the evidence of my imbecility. (The fact that I gave my daughter's mother a watch for three Christmases in a row will likely appear on my tombstone.)

I wandered aimlessly through the store, a broken man. But a Clearance sign caught my eye.

PVG Attempt #3. I was looking at a display of flower vases. But not those everyday glass spittoons. These were multicolored, blown-glass figurines shaped like a flower. What about a bouquet of real flowers delivered in this elegant, expensive-even-on-sale vase? It would reflect Thought, and my wife had told me once that flowers were always the right gift. Being artsy was way out of my comfort zone but surely—or at least more-than-likely—I had never done this before.

I dove into the abyss. I chose a vase using my trustworthy guide: bigger is better.

On V-Day minus one, I went by a florist with my vase treasure and arranged a bouquet of cut flowers all by myself. Of course, the florist lady did pick the type and the colors, told me how to place them, cut the stems, and tied on the bow. But other than petty details, it was all me. The floral instructor cooed over my choice, "What a lucky lady you have." But that remark brought an LOL out of Cupid.

The PVG Delivery. Successful deliveries of the Perfect Valentine Gift hinge on a "Creative Surprise." I chose the simple but safe "Breakfast Bonanza" technique: A carefully arranged V-Day display on the kitchen table set in place well before the queen of the home would awake.

The moment came! The creaking of the bedroom door, the padding of house shoes, the swinging door entry, and then . . . "Oh what a beautiful vase and what gorgeous flowers! You Thought of me!"

Ah, perfection.

Story Fifteen

Things That Prowl in the Night

In the classic tale, *The Wizard of Oz,* Dorothy and her friends fear lions, tigers and bears (oh my!). Dunnavant Valley doesn't have those creatures, but it does (or did) have a few predators that Dorothy should worry about.

The cougar is also known as mountain lion, puma, panther, or catamount. From *Alabama Wildlife Magazine,* "Historically this lion ranged from the Canadian Yukon to the southern tip of South America and, as might be expected, *Felis concolor* has been given more common names than any other mammal in the world."[1] This large cat is officially extirpated (dead and gone) from Alabama. Per the *Alabama Wildlife* article, the last bodily evidence was a cougar shot in Tuscaloosa County in 1956.

According to the experts, the only breeding colony in the eastern United States—a group big enough to propagate without inbreeding—is in south Florida. Panthers are still found in the wild in the western US, where they are commonly called mountain lions, and in private ownership in the east. A colony in the Smoky Mountains has been theorized but never confirmed.

Alabamians are avid outdoorsmen/women, hunters, anglers, loggers, and farmers. We have never kowtowed to "experts" professing to know our wildlife better than we do. Passionate arguments are made that panthers still roam our hills, though lacking are documented sightings or physical evidence like roadkill. Experts agree there is the possibility of western mountain lions roaming east or escaping from private zoos. In addition, according to the Cougarnet website, a male "Florida

- 79 -

panther" was confirmed in Georgia using DNA evidence. Other males from south Florida have been documented roaming hundreds of miles north.[2]

If they are not here now, they used to be because settlers named geographic features after them. The U.S. Geological Survey's Geographic Names Information System lists a number of place names using "panther" scattered across Alabama, e.g. North Fork Panther Creek in Lauderdale County and Panther Branch in Winston County.[3]

A cat that Dorothy would definitely have to look out for is the *Lynx rufus* or bobcat. This cat is so common in Alabama that it has a conservation concern level of "low." So that you know what to tell Dorothy: the adults are tawny or grayish brown with dark spots. A "big 'un" stands as high as two feet and weighs up to forty pounds. The name comes from its short or "bobbed" tail. It prefers deep woods but may show up in "urban edge" environments, like a Dunnavant Valley backyard.

A wild carnivore that I have definitely seen in my Dunnavant Valley backyard is the coyote (known to older movie theater patrons as "Wile E. Coyote"). This may be just me, but I don't remember coyotes being a pest in Alabama until the last ten years or so. The coyotes I have seen around our neighborhood are grayish brown and about the size of a middling dog but more skittish. Whenever I have seen one, it walks like it is on a mission, moving at a healthy pace but not running. A coyote doesn't stand around to allow a human a good look. Coyotes stalk prey both singly or as a pack. They would not hesitate to take a small domesticated animal like a cat, house dog, or poultry. Their howls at night from up in the hills are creepy. Not a fan.

Finally, we get to the crowd favorite, the black bear, *Ursus americanus*. The black bear is the official state mammal of Alabama by legislative decree on April 12, 2006. A strong population exists in the northeast Alabama counties of DeKalb, Cherokee, and Etowah. Auburn University has extensively studied a breeding colony of black bears near Mentone. A weaker population is found in southwest Alabama in Mobile, Washington, and Clarke counties. Male black bears are known to roam long distances in search of food or love. Confirmed sightings have been reported all over the state, in rural and urban areas, though I am not aware of any in the Dunnavant Valley.

It is fun to think of black bears as friendly. It may be fun to "ahh" over their cuteness. But black bears up-close and personal are not cute and not friendly. Male black bears average 250 pounds and are very powerful. Black bear attacks can be deadly. Stupid people feed bears. Don't stand between a bear and a food source, or get close to a sow and her cubs. Black bears are awesome and fascinating, but enjoy at a safe distance.

The Exotics

Dorothy would definitely not see this one coming: an emu. Yep, the smaller cousin of an ostrich. Several years ago an emu appeared in our neighborhood and our Facebook page blew up: "It's over here this morning," "it's on my street this afternoon," "it's so beautiful." Have you ever studied the face of an emu? Of course not, because they are UGLY. An emu would fit perfectly with the aliens at the Tatooine bar scene in *Star Wars*. The feathers are suitable for a can-can dancer, but otherwise an emu looks like it was pilfered from Dr. Frankenstein's dumpster.

I called the county animal control department. The personnel told me the bird had probably escaped or, more likely, been released from an emu farm. When the market for emu meat went bust, some emu ranchers simply opened their gates and walked away. The animal control experts said they would be willing to come and dispose of the misbegotten creature. One of their last comments was to advise that an emu will aggressively defend itself with its clawed feet. Think of the velociraptors in *Jurassic Park*.

I commented on the Facebook string of emu adoration that animal control offered to take care of the problem. I was told in no uncertain terms to backoff. One friend called to advise me I was "scaring the ladies."

In any case, the emu disappeared of its own volition after a few days of dazzling our residents. Fortunately, no one was disemboweled. Though the flightless bird has gone, I am stuck with a reputation as the neighborhood emu narc.

The last creature that Dorothy should be aware of is a legend. I have lived in Alabama for fifty spins around the sun and not until researching this book had I ever heard of this creature. It was like a secret magic book was cracked open just enough for me to be let into an inner circle (or maybe I googled, it's sorta foggy).

It is Alabama's bleached version of Big Foot. It is a humidity-tolerant Abominable Snowman. It is Moby Dick with legs. It is named with classic southern simplicity: The White Thang.

Cue *Twilight Zone* theme song: do-dum-dee-dah, do-dum-dee-dah.

The White Thang's habitat is Alabama including the Dunnavant Valley but sightings are claimed by many other locales. It is variously described as an eight-foot-tall, white-haired humanoid or as a shaggy white ape. Its origin is claimed to be an unknown species, like something from Loch Ness. I think it's more likely from a galaxy far, far away and long, long ago: the snow-white, dagger-fanged cave creature from the ice-planet Hoth (of *The Empire Strikes Back*). He's mad and looking for the limb that Luke Skywalker detached with his lightsaber. May the Force be with him.

A few things are for sure: the White Thang is fast, nimble, and formidable. Able to leap tall buildings in a single bound and outrun a Norfolk Southern locomotive. (I'm taking some liberty here, just to cover all the bases.)

Beware Dorothy, it's like some apparition from the *Outer Limits* (don't adjust your TV set, Windstream's out again). It's the White Thang!

Good luck Dorothy. And remember, sister, this ain't Kansas.

Story Sixteen

Firefighters Brotherhood

I'm not a fireman or first responder. My closest brush with emergency workers was a low-speed ride in an ambulance after an embarrassing fainting spell at a business meeting. Growing up, we had a chimney fire in our house that firefighters came and extinguished. Pretty exciting for a fifth grader. Other than those weak exposures, I have little background with those who come to our aid in a crisis. I suspect many residents of Dunnavant Valley are in the same position. And though we have little day-to-day thought about the men and women in the firehouse, when an emergency strikes their services will jump to the highest priority possible. Absolutely nothing else will matter.

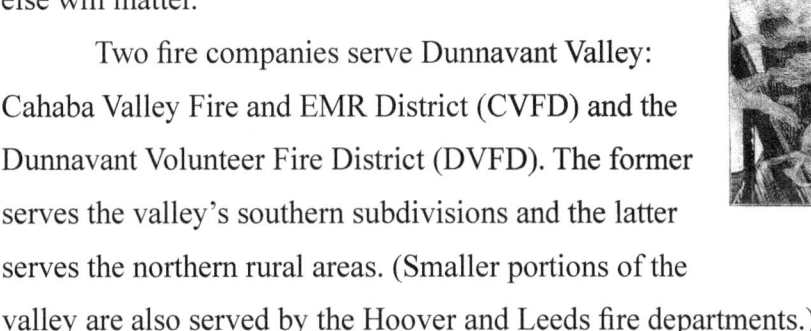

Two fire companies serve Dunnavant Valley: Cahaba Valley Fire and EMR District (CVFD) and the Dunnavant Volunteer Fire District (DVFD). The former serves the valley's southern subdivisions and the latter serves the northern rural areas. (Smaller portions of the valley are also served by the Hoover and Leeds fire departments.)

Besides fire suppression, the fire companies respond to a multitude of community needs: water leaks, trees down blocking roads, mountain rescues, and disasters like severe weather events. The majority of the calls are medical in nature and many of the firefighters are also trained and certified emergency medical technicians or paramedics.

In consideration of the Double Oak Mountain fire in 2022, both departments acquired all-terrain vehicles for use in fighting off-road fires. Indeed, the worst fire for DVFD burned the interior of the County Road 41N/101 loop in what was largely a forest fire.

A fire company's command structure and the peer-to-peer association is a quasi-military relationship. The rank system reflects the martial structure: sergeant, lieutenant, captain, chief. As in the military, discipline and training are vital. The resemblance to an army patrol—where each squad member covers a certain part of the perimeter—is very strong.

A fireman friend described the teamwork at a fire emergency. When the fire truck arrives, a firefighter is dropped off at the nearest fire plug and pulls connecting hose off the truck as the driver pulls forward. The truck itself has a tank but must be connected with the hydrant's "inexhaustible" supply to fight a large fire. The "apparatus operator" (the driver) positions the truck precisely to fit the circumstances. Another firefighter connects hose to the truck and begins dousing the fire, while the driver jumps down to work the truck's water pump. The "plug man" will catch up with the truck and either help the hose man, or set up to administer medical attention if victims are anticipated.

In the midst of an emergency, just as in a battle, each man or woman on the team must do his or her job. If any member fails, the team fails. Like soldiers, firefighters develop a unique fellowship through facing danger together and rescuing victims as a daily routine. They must depend on each other without hesitation. This trust becomes the cornerstone of a brotherhood.

A common drive binds together the brotherhood of firefighters. In his gripping autobiography, *20,000 Alarms,* firefighter Richard Hamilton explains how he came to understand this motivation early in his career:

> As my skills increased and I was able to do my job without concentrating a thousand percent on every move I made, I found I had time to think about what I was doing in another way. A larger

way. *Why* was I doing this? Why does any Fireman? . . . First of all, I knew I loved life very much myself. I loved my family, yes, and I loved the beauty of life itself. . . . Well, I thought, if *I* felt this way, a lot of other people must, too. They love life; they don't really want to lose their chance to live. . . So I made up my mind that anybody who wanted to live as much as I did would get a fair shake from me. I'd risk my life for theirs. I'd try as hard as I could. And if I lost my life in doing this, well, at least my family could hold up their heads and know that I had done something decent and worthwhile.[1]

The commonality of purpose described by Hamilton also exists between fire companies. Adjoining fire districts have mutual assistance agreements under which they come to the aid of a neighboring fire company should the emergency go beyond their neighbor's resources. The DVFD and CVFD have such an agreement. But their assistance to each other is not driven by words on a piece of paper. The Dunnavant fire company is all volunteer whereas the Cahaba Valley personnel are paid career firefighters, but they work together seamlessly.

The Cahaba Valley assists Dunnavant with medical transport—ambulances—and this greatly reduces the response time versus other options. Before Cahaba Valley stepped up, the average response time of an ambulance to an emergency in Dunnavant was forty-five minutes. The assistance of Cahaba Valley has cut that time to twenty minutes or less. This improvement can easily be the difference between life and death.

And when Double Oak Mountain caught fire in 2022, the Dunnavant fire department, and several other companies, came to the aid of Cahaba Valley.

Our culture today is divided on every imaginable plane. Commonality of purpose, and a selfless purpose at that, is exceedingly rare. Yet, purpose is what binds all emergency responders together. Daniel Byrne put it this way in Firehouse website, the go-to magazine for the firefighting industry:

Every day firefighters leave the station rushing towards the unknown, not knowing if they will return, simply because Ms. Smith is in need of help. Suddenly, Ms. Smith, the stranger, becomes more important than your own health and safety, more important than your children and family, more important than your future. You expose yourself to extreme risk to save Ms. Smith who is a woman you never met, and you hold your ground as the world disintegrates around you, not only for Ms. Smith, but because the person next to you who shares the same desire for Ms. Smith's well-being is counting on you to be there.[2]

Byrne went on to say, "That desire, that pursuit, and that unquenchable need to fill it, is what called you [the firefighter] to this career and to the front doors of the firehouse your first rookie day." Firefighters choose to run *toward* the fire—the accident, the bleeding, the pain, the trauma, the fear, the panic, the danger—rather than run *from it*. They are uniquely connected because of this voluntary choice.

The selflessness of first responders shines like a beacon of assurance that all is not lost in our loud, misguided society. May we be generous in our support.

May God protect you.

Story Seventeen

Shoal Creek

As I was gathering research for this book, someone asked, "So what is Dunnavant Valley known for?" I struggled to answer. It contains no historic sites, iron forges, or famous homes as celebrated in other parts of the county. No nationally recognized politicians, military leaders, or celebrities have originated from the valley (though some may have moved here since).

However, there is an establishment that has made the valley famous far beyond the ridges. It is nationally and internationally recognized. It is known as Shoal Creek.

How does a vision like Shoal Creek appear? For Hall Thompson, it was born of his love for the game of golf, and interest in a country club and golf course that attained a superior level of excellence. The vision became more that a wistful desire when a business associate asked what he really wanted to do in life. Already highly successful in business, he said he'd like to build a superior golf course. His colleague responded: then do it.

Thompson's first step was to consult with his friend Hugh Daniel, CEO of Daniel Corporation, another highly successful Birmingham businessman, about his desire to build an extraordinary golf course. Thompson and Daniel agreed on the purchase of approximately 1,500 acres that Daniel owned in Dunnavant Valley at the foot of Double Oak Mountain. Prior to Daniel, the land had been owned by Josh Oden of the Alabama Mineral Land Company. Before Oden, it was railroad land: The pines were harvested for ties and timbers by the railways of Selma (Alabama) and Rome and Dalton (Georgia).[1]

The namesake of the future golf course, Shoal Creek, starts as a mountain spring in the southern part of the property and then winds its way across the site.

The woodlands canopy is made of sourwood, oak, hickory, sweetgum, maple, and pine. The woodlands are carpeted with an understory of oakleaf hydrangea, mountain laurel, and native hollies.[2] Deep and green in the summer, the forests become a palette of color in the fall.

The agreement with Daniel also included land adjacent to Daniel Corporation's Greystone development. Thompson built an access road on this property from US Highway 280 along the slopes of Oak Mountain to Overton Gap then down to the valley floor and an intersection with Dunnavant Valley Road. This became the Hugh Daniel Drive we know today.

Now enters the second individual integral to fulfilling Thompson's vision: Jack Nicklaus. By 1981, *Golf Magazine* reported that Nicklaus had "dominated his sport longer and with more certainty than any other athlete in modern history."[3] With five PGA Player-of-the-Year awards he was the most successful golf professional in the field. Nicklaus was also well into a second career as a golf course architect and resort community developer. The *Golf* article reported his $3.6 million winnings as a golfer paled in comparison to the $300 million in gross revenue from designing, building and servicing courses and in resort development and land sales.

However, backup for a moment to 1974 when Hall Thompson asked Nicklaus to visit his 1,500 acres. Nicklaus had collaborated on a number of courses but had yet to solo on a course development. It was a big step for both men to engage in an agreement to develop Shoal Creek.

Work began on the course, and also on the clubhouse and associated structures. The *Golf* article quotes Nicklaus on the course installation process, "During the construction, I make periodic visits. If it's a heavily treed course, I walk it carefully, making sure the center lines are cut accurately, and that not too much chopping is done. After all, it takes 100 years to grow a tree, five minutes to chop it down, and another 100 years for it to grow back. Then I check the earth shaping, the cuts and fills, the lakes, the shaping of the bunkers, and the fine grading, at which time we put in the irrigation and shape the greens. Later, the grass is planted and rolled. I'm involved in every step."[4] Nicklaus arranged the course to take full advantage of the stream of its name; the waters of Shoal Creek and its feeder streams are involved in half of the holes.[5]

In November of 1977, the first round of golf teed off at Shoal Creek. Acclaim for the new course came soon and was stunning. *Golf Digest* ranked it among the top fifty courses in America. *Golf Magazine* rated it 26th in the world.[6]

The course's greatness was confirmed when Shoal Creek was selected to hold the 1984 PGA Championship. The PGA Championship is one of the four annual golf "majors" along with the US Open, the British Open (or simply The Open), and the Masters at Augusta National. Shoal Creek was the youngest course to ever host a major.

The PGA Championship brought world-class golf participation and competition to Alabama with all the associated benefits. This year, 2024, is the 40th anniversary of the initial tournament at Shoal Creek.

A history of notable tournaments include:

- 1984 PGA Championship (winner Lee Trevino)
- 1986 USGA Amateur Championship (winner Buddy Alexander)
- 1990 PGA Championship (winner Wayne Grady)
- 1993-1996 Jerry Pate Intercollegiate (Stanford University won in 1994 led by Tiger Woods)
- 2008 US Junior Amateur Championship (winner Cameron Peck)
- 2010 Southern Amateur Championship (winner Alex Carpenter)
- 2011-2015 Regions Tradition (a major on the PGA Tour Champions)
- 2018 US Women's Open Championship (winner Ariya Jutanugarn)
- 2023 PGA Works Collegiate Championship (joint host with Bent Brook)

Shoal Creek was renovated in 2016 with Jack Nicklaus again providing consulting services. After his start at Shoal Creek, Nicklaus led the design and development of dozens of courses both in the US and abroad. During his professional golf career Nicklaus won eighteen major championships (three more than Tiger Woods) and a total of 118 victories around the world. He sank twenty-one hole-in-one shots. Jack Nicklaus is considered one of the greatest golfers of all time.[7]

Shoal Creek is, of course, more than a golf course: It is one of the premier estate communities in the southeast. The Williamsburg-style clubhouse, town hall, cottages, and green "commons" exude dignity and grace. The town hall is a local polling place (and the location of my daughter's wedding). The Shoal Creek residential community enjoys the peace and beauty of the undisturbed woodlands with the Double Oak ridgeline as a backdrop.

Hall Thompson was inducted into the Alabama Sports Hall of Fame in 1987 as the first ever Distinguished Alabama Sportsman. The founder of Shoal Creek passed away on October 27, 2010, at age 87.

Hall Thompson's vision lives on in Shoal Creek.

Story Eighteen

Preserving the Mountains

Let's peer down with a red-tailed hawk as it cruises the valley.

Beginning at The Narrows community, adjacent to the gorge of Yellow Leaf Creek, the hawk's flight crosses the business area along US Highway 280 and the headquarters of the Cahaba Valley Fire District. Hidden in the woods beside 280, just about where Yellow Leaf Creek flows invisibly under the four-lane, is the Pierce Memorial Cemetery (also known as Shady Grove Cemetery) which contains some of the oldest gravesites in the valley. The southern end of the valley shelters homes and neighborhoods and the hawk spies on hikers enjoying the Dunnavant Valley Greenway.

Continuing northeast through the valley, his flight crosses Dunnavant Valley Park. Somewhere in the woods behind the park is the spray of a slender waterfall as it tumbles down the hillside from the mountain springs that feed it.

Next, past the short surviving piece of Old Dunnavant Valley Road, is the retail oasis adjacent to and across the street from Mt Laurel. Besides stores and eateries, it also contains a Cahaba Valley fire station, Double Oak Community Church, the Mt Laurel Library, and an acre or so of greenspace. A similar community center is the essence of every rural town in Alabama. The hawk flies on oblivious to man's conveniences.

- 91 -

Past Mt Laurel, somewhere in the Double Oak foothills, are the headwaters of Shoal Creek, located in the development that adopted its name. The hawk banks to the left to glimpse the headwaters of the North Fork of Yellow Leaf Creek emanating from a lake in Greystone Farms. The headwaters of these two streams are less than a half mile apart, yet they wonderfully defy gravity: Yellow Leaf flows *south* toward The Narrows, and Shoal Creek flows *north* toward Dunnavant.

Past the intersection of Dunnavant Valley Road and Hugh Daniel Drive, the developments gradually thin out. The cousin of falcons passes over the stately entrance to Shoal Creek and the majestic fairways walked by the legends of golf. He stretches out his full four-foot wingspan, red tail spread in an arc, as he glides soundlessly over the wooded shores of Great Pine, Smyer, Hollybrook, and Wehapa lakes. The hawk wings over Ball Park Lane, where churches once gathered for softball games, and then over Kendrick Family Cemetery and Pleasant Ridge Baptist Church.

There is a roller-coaster hollow in the terrain at Lake Providence after which the bird of prey must beat the air to avoid the transmission lines spanning the valley. He calls aloud to express his annoyance with this intrusion into the sky he owns. Without a hint of curiosity, he passes over the Winding Stair street sign marking a country lane that winds into the hills.

A bit further, as it has for some 160 years or more, the valley embraces the community named for the Dunn & Avant Commissary. At the corner of Dunnavant Valley Road and Highway 25 is the primary station of the Dunnavant Volunteer Fire District. Our hawk wings to the left, to pass over the Dunnavant Community Center, the building the community built to replace its elementary school after the winter fire of 1961.

Our hawk wings over Alabama Highway 25 and the Norfolk Southern track which cross the valley from mountain to mountain. John Henry Dabney, former slave, was on the crew that carved the tunnels with steel and dynamite through solid rock 137 years ago. The mountains bear the tunnel wounds without complaining, but silently ask for no more.

The valley does not stop here but continues past Sand Ridge and, not much further as a hawk flies, the silent aviator crosses over lonely Harmony Church Cemetery, cut off by an iron gate from its descendants. Still the rich forests of the valley roll on below the piercing eyes of the hawk, past Hillhouse Lake, and into St. Clair County.

This graceful flight through the valley has been defined to the north by the ridges of Oak Mountain, and to the south by Double Oak Mountain. From Oak Mountain State Park to the St. Clair county line, Dunnavant Valley hosts the highest crest on either ridge: Double Oak Mountain pushes up to an elevation just over 1,500 feet above sea level behind Shoal Creek. At certain points on the crest of the ridge, it's possible to see all the way to Shades Mountain in Vestavia.

Dunnavant Valley shares with the state and county parks the honor of preserving the southernmost crests of the Appalachian Mountains. The valley lies in the Alabama physiological region known as Valley and Ridge and in the sixty-mile-long subregion known as the Coosa Ridges. The serene, forested ridges frame the valley's beauty. With its forested ridges intact, the Dunnavant Valley is a natural Cinderella, underappreciated but, oh, so captivating.

But the beauty of these ridges is unprotected and vulnerable.

Preserving a Mountain

In early 2015, a small group of Dunnavant Valley residents approached the Freshwater Land Trust, a nonprofit conservation organization, about an opportunity to preserve a two-mile stretch of Double Oak Mountain. The concept was to purchase 225 acres of ridge property from the Smyer family to be owned and managed by the Trust in order to preclude development in perpetuity.

The group could have been prompted by current land development techniques that require slopes, hills, and ridges to be deforested and leveled.

These techniques are good for the economics of the developer, but transfigure forever the topography of the land. The natural, undisturbed watershed and forest canopy are sacrificed.

> I grew up camping and hiking in the Great Smoky Mountains National Park. I appreciate the drama of the Rockies, but I love the blue-misted forests of the Appalachian Mountains.
>
> Later, in the mid 1970s, I worked in Appalachia near Middlesboro, Kentucky, for a coal mining company. I was in the loadout facilities, not in the mines, but from the company helicopter I saw the results of strip mining. The seams of coal were in uniform layers running at a fixed elevation through the hills and ridgelines of the mountains. To get to the coal, the forested ridges of the Appalachians were systematically leveled into artificial flat-topped mesas.
>
> At the time, as a young engineer, I tried to rationalize in my mind that what I saw happening was good for the economy. I am no longer so sure. The strip mining practices that I witnessed in eastern Kentucky come to mind when I see land development practices today.

The Trust's interest was piqued by Double Oak Mountain's treasure trove of biodiversity in both flora and wildlife. The mountain's preservation would fit squarely into the Trust's objective to "conserve and care for environmentally significant land and water throughout central Alabama. . ."[1]

The challenge in preserving the ridgeline was financial. The Smyer family was prepared to sell the property at a significant discount to the appraised value, and the Trust had secured a considerable philanthropic grant, as well as pledges from communities and individuals in the valley. However, a substantial balance remained. The Trust asked the three neighborhood associations located below the proposed purchase—Stonegate Farms, Smyer, and Hollybrook—if their members would close the gap.

The officers of the three homeowners' associations formed committees and set to work notifying their members of the opportunity and soliciting pledges. Several members gave generous foundational gifts, and many members gave sacrificially. Remarkably, in a matter of a few months, the needed funds had been pledged with a majority of the associations' members contributing. The board of the Trust subsequently voted to approve the purchase, the project was financed, the purchase was closed, and the property was permanently preserved.

Today, the protected portion of the ridgeline runs northeast roughly from the border of the Shoal Creek community to the border of the Lake Wehapa community. The unspoiled mountain reflects the stewardship of this picturesque corner of Creation by the citizens of Dunnavant Valley.

Author's note: Shelby County has recently secured significant tracts of Oak and Double Oak Mountains for public use. As a result of these efforts, a portion of our ridgelines will remain pristine for our posterity. However, miles of Shelby County's ridgelines are not so preserved.

The Dunnavant Valley Small Area Plan

In 2012, as a derivative of the county's comprehensive planning, the Development Services Department of Shelby County was directed to work with the public on a focused study of Dunnavant Valley. The study was to address issues facing the valley and then formulate a vision and a "list of goals, objectives and implementation strategies" to benefit the valley's residents, stakeholders, and visitors.

A Steering Committee was formed based on prior public participation and suggestions from staff, local organizations, and residents. The objective was to "create a fair representation of members" from throughout the valley. At the kickoff meeting in August 2012, the Steering Committee was tasked with the promotion of the plan, identifying issues, and defining goals and strategies.

Subsequently, the community at large was invited—by means of local periodicals and notices to homeowners' associations—to attend several public workshops. Attendees were asked to identify and prioritize issues in topics such as land use, community design, transportation, facilities and services, economic development, natural and cultural resources, and housing.

The top dozen issues identified in the workshops were the following:

Issues	Number of votes
Bike lanes on Dunnavant Valley Road to remove cyclists from traffic	28
No apartments or multifamily dwellings	21
Preserve the undisturbed Oak and Double Oak Mountain ridges	19
No annexation	16
Enhance police presence by adding sheriff's office substation	15
Limit large commercial development (no "big boxes")	15
Do not want another grocery store with a pharmacy	13
No more zoning–it encourages mass development	11
Need to enforce / reduce the speed limit along Dunnavant Valley Road	9
Add pedestrian pathways along Dunnavant Valley Road	7
Need to install pedestrian connections between neighborhoods	7
Preservation of viewscapes/reduction in sign advertisements	7

The Steering Committee took the community workshop input and developed goals for Dunnavant Valley. These goals were expanded and consolidated into a final report, a copy of which is in the Mt Laurel Library.

The final report of the Dunnavant Valley Small Area Plan is rich with maps and technical data, but the bottom line is in the chapter at the end containing "Goals, Objectives, and Strategies." The list includes forty specific strategies with a timeline, an advocate, and a detailed description for each one—twenty pages of text. It is an impressive body of work that was thoroughly vetted by the county's professional staff and residents of the valley.

Without going into painstaking detail, the strategies address issues related to the greenway, traffic, sheriff offices, cyclists, railroads, ball fields, commercial sprawl, scenic highways, wildflowers, conservation education, and creation of a district to protect the ridges. This is just a sample but indicates the broad scope. The strategies are worthwhile and still relevant.

As much work as the study entailed, implementation is the true challenge. Advocates for the strategies include government entities—Shelby County, Alabama Department of Transportation, the City of Hoover, and the Legislative Delegation—as well as private entities—Norfolk Southern and Mt Laurel. Some fifteen of the strategies are simply left to the "Residents."

It's admirable that certain goals have been accomplished or partially accomplished. But only a fraction have been addressed.

The Dunnavant Valley Small Area Plan was ratified by the county commission on August 11, 2014. This year, 2024, is the plan's tenth anniversary. After a decade of years, I would submit that all of the goals remaining to be accomplished have only the residents as advocates. We cannot blame government bodies or corporations if we don't stand up and say how much we care.

After all, we are the stewards of all we have been given.

A Parting Thought

The valley has a long history of individuals with vision: the settlers who carved homes out of the wilderness, the Dunnavant community who rebuilt their school, the neighborhoods who preserved their portion of Double Oak Mountain, and the world-size vision of Shoal Creek.

Does the valley still inspire? The Dunnavant mother rebuilding her children's school gave us a worthy example: if we desire something badly—if it's life-giving for ourselves, our family, or our community—how hard will we work to achieve it?

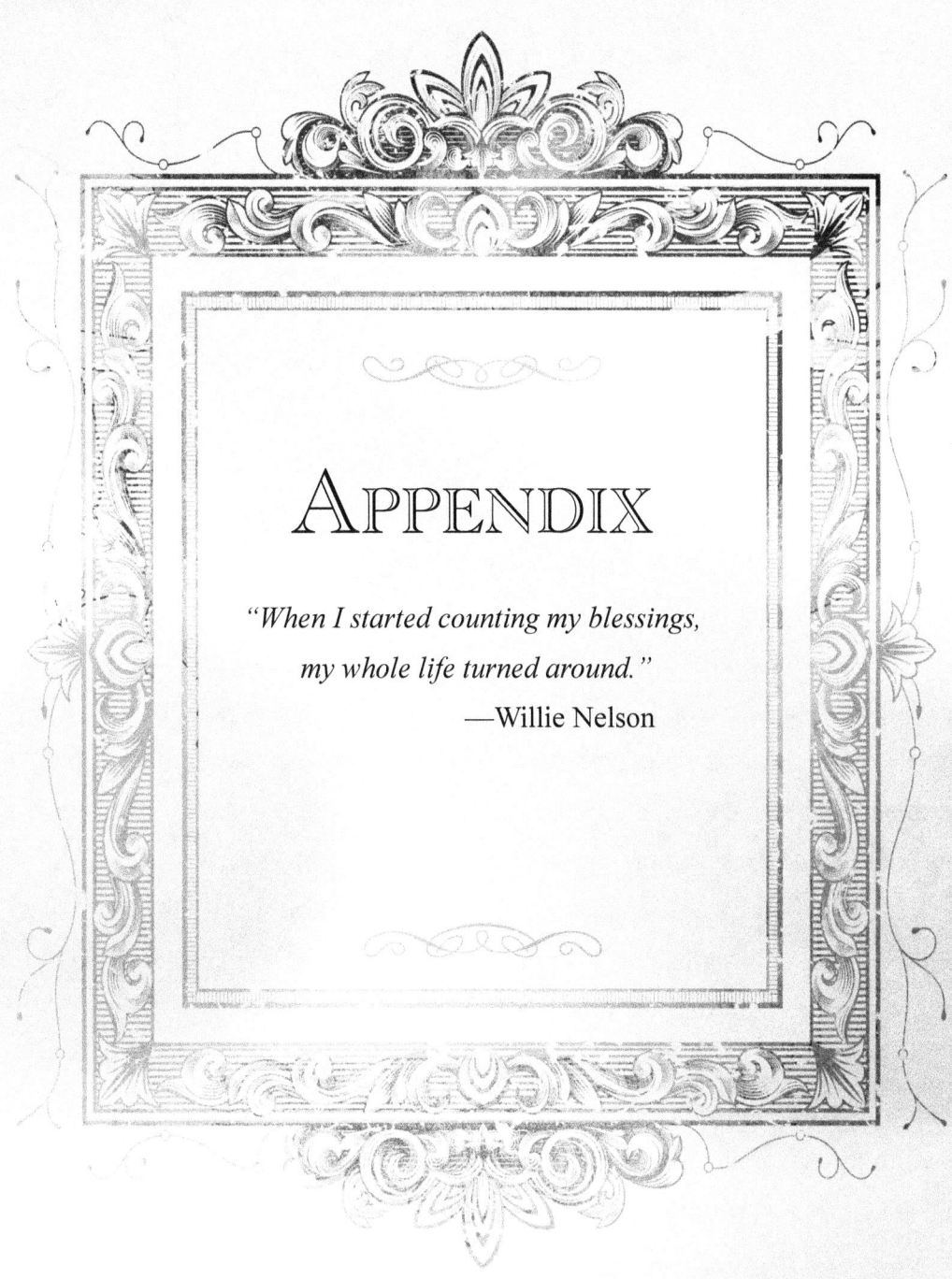

Appendix

*"When I started counting my blessings,
my whole life turned around."*
—Willie Nelson

Walking in His Shoes

An excerpt from Sojourn on the Veld, *a memoir of South Africa, recounting work and ministry in South Africa during the apartheid era. Published 2022, Insight Press.*

The Bophuthatswana government [a tribal homeland in South Africa] had an unwritten policy that government workers should employ a domestic servant. The logic was that government employees were relatively well off and should help the unemployed. We never saw a formal mandate, but it was made clear through various channels that employing domestic help was a non-negotiable expectation.

When Joe, Mike, and I moved into our government house, we hired Dorcas as our housekeeper. Some friends of the ministry had recommended Dorcas, and she was indeed a good worker. She came faithfully, on time, two days a week to wash our clothes and clean our house. She renamed us "Joey, Marks, and Bully," and we learned to respond promptly when our names were called.

Dorcas wore a traditional long black dress and head wrap, so we had no idea if she was gray-haired. It was impossible to tell her age apart from her wrinkles, which indicated she was old.

She was respectful (sort of) because we were her employers but otherwise had no apprehension of any authority owed to us because we were Americans, or Jesus followers, or any trait we could muster up. Further, as bachelors, we started at a deficit respect-wise. Why had we not earned the cattle to pay *lobola*, the bride price? Shameful.

We occasionally discarded old clothing or household items, but we did not need to look for a charity: Dorcas took all of our old belongings as if they were some sort of treasure. She even took my worn-out pair of brown men's shoes with the right sole flapping at the toe.

Over time, we learned that Dorcas had a son.

It was sometime later, on a Saturday morning, that a young Tswana man knocked on our front door. We opened the door, and the young man stepped in and immediately took a seat in one of our living room chairs. We sat down as well, smiled, and patiently waited. We had learned that this no-introduction-make-yourself-at-home behavior was a perfectly acceptable African entrance. The best thing to do was to take a seat and nod pleasantly, knowing an explanation would come with time, and then to prepare tea. The young man was dressed in a buttoned coat and a tie, which were old but obviously his best clothes. After some minutes the silence was broken.

"I am Dorcas's son, Joseph."

"Oh!" we exclaimed in unison, and then we exchanged greetings in Setswana, and English too, since it was obvious that Dorcas's son had a considerably better grasp of English than Dorcas. We proceeded to heat the teapot and explore conversation. He was in high school and hoped to graduate soon. We talked about soccer, church choirs, and other topics that were interesting to a Tswana youth of his age.

It was during Joseph's explanation to Joe of which soccer team was the best that I happened to look down at his feet. I noticed that he was wearing a well-worn pair of brown men's shoes with the right sole flapping at the toe.

I've heard it said that all Americans are rich in the eyes of the world because even our poorest live better than the vast majority of the world. I've also heard it said that an American who makes $35,000 per year is in the top ten percent of the world population in terms of income. But cold statistics can never humble as much as meeting a young man in his best clothes, who is proudly wearing the shoes you discarded as worn out.

On one occasion, we went to see where Dorcas lived. It was a traditional red mud house with a thatched roof in one of the outlying villages from Montshiwa. I recorded in my journal:

She was excited to see us but embarrassed that she wasn't dressed well . . . Seeing her place helped us understand a little better why she is sometimes so defensive & so prideful of our place. Makes me appreciate the way God has blessed us too.

Our concrete-block government house was humble by Western standards, but a few miles away, our hardworking housekeeper lived in the third world. And even Dorcas in her thatched-roof house with a corn plot as a front yard was better off than the destitute in the shanty-filled barrio we had visited in Mexico and the squatter camps that existed in other parts of South Africa. I mused in my journal:

In the States, poverty was in pockets and not so untreatable. Here poverty is the norm and is so vast that it can only be dealt with in pockets . . .

When one sees such poor standards of living, and if you know the character of the people living there, one can only conclude that we Americans have scarcely a hint, only a faint conception, of how richly God has blessed our land.

Endnotes

Introduction
1. Patrick Thompson, Trees Company LLC, December 1, 2023.

The Brits Pick a Fight
1. Ove Jensen, "Battle of Horseshoe Bend," *The Encyclopedia of Alabama*, July 12, 2024; encyclopediaofalabama.org/article/battle-of-horseshoe-bend/.

Alabama's Land Rush
1. *Alabama Bessemer Sheet, Scale 1:125,000*, US Geological Survey, Edition April 1892, reprinted February 1900.
2. *Historic Roads and Trails*, State of Alabama Highway Department, Department of Archives and History, 1975. Map Sales Office, Montgomery, Alabama.
3. "People," *Horseshoe Bend: National Military Park Alabama*, National Park Service, April 27, 2022; www.nps.gov/hobe/learn/historyculture/people.htm. Author's Note: This site has links to the muster rolls for the forces serving with General Jackson at Horseshoe Bend.
4. "Shelby County, Early Settlement and History," *History of Alabama and Dictionary of Alabama*. Publisher and author unknown. A hardcopy of an excerpt is located at the Shelby County Historical Society.
5. Marilyn David Barefield (compiler), *Old Tuskaloosa Land Office Records & Military Warrants 1821-1855* (Easley, SC: Southern Historical Press, Inc., 1984), viii-ix.
6. Gregory Boyd, *The Family Maps of Shelby County, Alabama* (Norman, Oklahoma: Arphax Publishing Co., 2007).
7. Barefield, various pages.
8. Boyd, *The Family Maps of Shelby County, Alabama*.
9. "Life in Appalachia," *Cumberland Gap: National Historical Park KY TN VA*, National Park Service, December 16, 2020; www.nps.gov/cuga/learn/historyculture/life-in-appalachia.htm.
10. *A Few Facts About Shelby County.* Unpublished, author unknown. A hardcopy is located at the Shelby County Historical Society.

Florida Short Route
1. *Birmingham Water Works Company (1887),* Historical marker erected by the Birmingham-Jefferson Historical Society 1996. (Located on Pump House Road adjacent to the Cahaba Pump Station.)
2. *Alabama Bessemer Sheet, Scale 1:125,000*, US Geological Survey, Edition September 1890.
3. David F. Moore, "Say Goodbye to the Narrows and a colorful page in history," *Shelby County Reporter*, December 3, 1981.
4. David F. Moore, "Narrows will be remembered," *Shelby County Reporter*, December 10, 1981.
5. E. A. Turner, *Road Map of Shelby County Alabama* (Birmingham: Whitson Map and Blueprint Co., 1925); alabamamaps.ua.edu/historicalmaps/counties/shelby/shelby.html.
6. *Shelby County Reporter*, December 3, 1981.
7. Thomas F. Hill, "4-laning Highway 280 to detour around the scenic Narrows gorge," *The Birmingham News*, December 2, 1977.
8. State Highway Department, *State Road Map of Alabama* (Montgomery: State Highway Department, 1930); alabamamaps.ua.edu/historicalmaps/stateroads/index.html.
9. "The Short Route to Florida," *280 Living*, August 2014, A18-19.
10. General Drafting Company, Inc., *State Road Map of Alabama* (New York: General Drafting Company, 1934); alabamamaps.ua.edu/historicalmaps/stateroads/index.html.

11. *Shelby County Reporter,* December 3, 1981.

12. Jackie Romine," The Short Route to Florida," *280 Living,* August 2014.

13. "U.S. 280," *AA Roads,* August 22, 2022; www.aaroads.com/guides/us-280-al/.

Dunnavant Past

1. Bill and Sue Tubbs, *Shelby County, Alabama Ancestral Homesteads* (Jasper, Alabama: Bill & Sue Tubbs, 2001).

2. "Surname Files," *The Shelby County Historical Society Museum & Archives*; https://www.shelbycountyhistory.com/surname-files.

3. Alabama Department of Archives and History, *Civil War Service Database;* archives.alabama.gov/research/CivilWarService.aspx.

4. The Shelby County Heritage Book Committee, *The Heritage of Shelby County, Alabama* (Clanton: Heritage Publishing Consultants, Inc., 1999), 17.

5. *General Highway Map of Shelby County, Alabama* (2011), Alabama Department of Transportation; digital.archives.alabama.gov/digital/api/singleitem/image/maps/4996/default.jpg.

6. *Shelby County, Highway Functional Classification,* Alabama Department of Transportation; www.dot.state.al.us/maps/pdf/surveyMapping/HFC/regec/59-Shelby.pdf.

7. Rand McNally & Co., *Index Atlas of the World, Alabama* (Chicago: Rand McNally & Co., 1998); cartweb.geography.ua.edu/.

8. *Find A Grave*; www.findagrave.com/cemetery/

9. *The Heritage of Shelby County*, 15.

10. Dunnavant spur according to local tradition. Chelsea spur mentioned in *Shelby County Reporter,* December 3, 1981.

11. Bill Carey, "Before the national park, large parts of the Smokies were clear-cut," *The Tennessee Magazine,* October 1, 2014; www.tnmagazine.org/before-the-national-park-large-parts-of-the-smokies-were-clear-cut/

12. Camma Cook, *Camma Gabrialle Holladay Cook: A Personal History* (Tallahassee, FL: Personal Histories LLC, 1999), 8.

13. "Shelby County, Post Offices and Towns," *History of Alabama and Dictionary of Alabama.*

14. Don Brown, "School's ashes seem like symbol of death to Shelby community," *The Birmingham News,* October 1, 1961, 26.

15. Holly Giles, "Pioneer Culture: Family Relationships," *The Giles Frontier*; www.thegilesfrontier.com/pioneer-culture-family-relationships/.

16. Jerrold Parker, *Annual Parker BBQ in the Grove 1997*. Unpublished, courtesy Peggy Johnson, Dunnavant.

The Winding Stair Trail

1. *Sidney Word Lee (1864-1944)*, Historical marker erected by the Alabama Historical Association, 2011. (Located on Highway 25 on the east side of Wyatts Gap.)

2. *Alabama Vandiver Quadrangle, Scale 1:62,500,* US Geological Survey, Edition June 1908, reprinted 1942.

3. *State Road Map of Alabama,* 1930.

4. Alabama Highway Department, *Alabama Highways* (Montgomery: Alabama State Highway Department, 1955).

5. Alabama Highway Department, *Official 1957 Alabama Highway Map* (Montgomery: Alabama State Highway Department, 1957).

By the Light of the Moon

1. Walter Harper, "Some Interesting History Of Shelby County," *The Shelby County Sun*, September 17, 1914. *Author's note: A hardcopy of this article is located at the Shelby County Historical Society, Columbiana, Alabama.*
2. "Whiskey Prices Increase Says Birmingham," *Shelby County Reporter*, December 20, 1928. Language partially reconstructed.
3. *Shelby County Reporter*, December 10, 1981
4. *Shelby County Reporter*, December 3, 1981
5. *Shelby County Reporter*, December 3, 1981
6. *Shelby County Reporter*, December 10, 1981

Highways of Iron

1. "The first automobile: 1885-1886," *Mercedes Benz Group*; group.mercedes-benz.com/company/tradition/company-history/1885-1886.html.
2. "Proposal for Tunnels", *The Daily American, Nashville*, October 29, 1886, 8. *Author's note:* The Daily American, Nashville *newspaper was a precursor to* The Tennessean.
3. *The Weekly Iron Age,* June 21, 1888 (from *Leeds, Her Story*, courtesy Leeds Historical Society).

John Henry's Race

1. S. Flannagan, "The Legend of John Henry Explained," *Grunge*, December 9, 2020, 12:50 PM EST; www.grunge.com/292440/the-legend-of-john-henry-explained/.
2. John Garst, "On the Trail of the Real John Henry," *History News Network*; www.historynewsnetwork.org/article/on-the-trail-of-the-real-john-henry.
3. "The Legend of John Henry: Talcott, WV," *New River Gorge National Park & Preserve West Virginia*, National Park Service, January 22, 2020; www.nps.gov/neri/planyourvisit/the-legend-of-john-henry-talcott-wv.htm.

Sounds of the Valley

1. "Norfolk Southern Railway," *Wikipedia: The Free Encyclopedia,* September 4, 2024; en.wikipedia.org/wiki/Norfolk_Southern_Railway.
2. "Railroad Safety: Train Horns and Grade Crossing Signals," *Union Pacific: Building America,* September 22, 2020; www.up.com/customers/track-record/tr101620-train-safety-horns-signals.htm.

Past Yet Present

1. Frances Saiia, "Shelby County History," *The Shelby County Advertiser*, June 6, 1974. *Author's note: A hardcopy of this article is located at the Shelby County Historical Society, Columbiana, Alabama.* The Shelby County Advertiser *ceased operations in 1976 and its successor* The Shelby County News *ceased operations in 1980. After researching the Library of Congress online, the author concluded the copyright for this article is orphaned.*

Dunnavant Redux

1. *The Birmingham News,* February 1, 1961.
2. *Heritage of Shelby County,* 71.
3. "Correction: Their school didn't die," *The Birmingham News,* August 26, 1962, A-31.
4. Bert Seaman, "Newest town on the map," *Shelby County Reporter*, May 18, 1994.

Things That Prowl in the Night

1. "Cougar—Alabama's Native Lion," *Alabama Wildlife Magazine,* Winter 1999; www.easterncougarnet.org/Cougar-Alabama's%20Native%20Lion.htm.
2. *The Cougar Network: Using Science to Understand Cougar Behavior, Southeast,* circa 2007; www.cougarnet.org/southeast.html.
3. "Domestic Names," *US Board on Geographic Names,* USGS Geographic Names Information System; www.usgs.gov/us-board-on-geographic-names/domestic-names.

Firefighters Brotherhood

1. Lt. Richard Hamilton with Charles N. Barnard, *20,000 Alarms* (New York: Playboy paperbacks, 1975) 103-104.

2. Daniel Byrne, "Finding the Guardians of Your Brotherhood," *Firehouse*, November 14, 2014; www.firehouse.com/careers-education/article/12018286/keeping-the-brotherhood-of-firefighting-alive.

Shoal Creek

1. "Shoal Creek, What a Golf Course Should Be," *Southern Living*, Southern Living, Inc, February 1984.

2. *Southern Living,* February 1984.

3. George Peper, "Jack's Other Career," *Golf Magazine,* March 1981.

4. *Golf Magazine*, March 1981.

5. *Southern Living,* February 1984.

6. Jim Warters, "Alabama Gold," *PGA Magazine,* August 1984.

7. "About Jack, Professional Statistics," *Nicklaus Companies*; nicklaus.com/about-jack/professional-stats/.

Preserving the Mountains

1. "About Us," *Freshwater Land Trust;* freshwaterlandtrust.org/who-we-are/about-us/.

About the Author

Bill Norton is a seasoned observer of life in the South. He grew up in Nashville, Tennessee, attended high school in Donelson, Memphis, and Collierville, and finished high school in Roanoke, Alabama. His work included small town and big city stints across the South, as well as Alabama. Bill holds an engineering degree from Auburn University and masters degrees from the University of Alabama at Birmingham and Vanderbilt University. Bill was a manager with the Southern Company for thirty-five years.

Bill and his wife, Lori, have lived in Shelby County for nearly forty years, and twenty of those years have been spent on their farmette in the Dunnavant Valley. Bill is a past president of his neighborhood association, served on the steering committee of the Dunnavant Valley Small Area Plan, is a past chairman of the Shelby County Planning Commission, and currently serves on the CVFD Community Advisory Group. Bill and Lori are members of The Church at Brook Hills.

Bill's first book, a memoir entitled *Sojourn on the Veld,* was published in 2022 by Insight Press. It recounts Bill's work and ministry in South Africa during the apartheid era. Find it at Briarwood Christian Bookstore in Birmingham or with most online booksellers.

www.ingramcontent.com/pod-product-compliance
Lightning Source LLC
LaVergne TN
LVHW081451060526
838201LV00050BA/1765